1086986 4

A Book Every Married Couple Should Read

Here is an eminently sensible book on Christian marriage. It is both readable and realistic. Although straightforwardly admitting that no marriage is perfect and that there are no quick fixes or magic fomulae, it nevertheless offers a host of working principles well worth pondering and applying. Brian Nystrom's insights into the dynamics of marriage—both good and bad—are illuminating, constructive and badly needed.

Catherine Clark Kroeger Author and Co-Founder of Christians for Biblical Equality

"No marriage is exempt from entropy," Brian Nystrom points out. And that is why his book touches sensitive nerves: Everyone will find people they recognize (only too well) in the pages of this thought-provoking book. Ordinary People–Extraordinary Marriages is an invaluable help to discover what things destroy love in a marriage. And even better yet, what to do about them. A 'must read' book for all who are married or think they ever might.

Dr. Joy Elasky Fleming

Brian Nystrom uses his insights in psychology and biblical teachings to help readers develop healthy marriages and healthy emotional and mental lives. This volume includes insightful, helpful material not found in most other books on marriage.

Alvera Mickelson, Author/former teacher at Bethel College and Seminary/co-founder of

Christians for Biblical Equality

This is no ordinary book—it is indeed Extra Ordinary. With almost half of all marriages—Christian marriage included—ending in divorce, we must re-examine our notions of what makes a marriage work. What exactly does submission in marriage mean? There are thousands of marriage books with millions of suggestions, but Brian Nystrom shares a novel insight into God's real design for marriage. He uses personal stories from his vast experience and the reader is able to relate with the characters and their situations. Practical application follows. I wish that everyone who is married or about to be married could read this book.

Guy R. Doud, National Teacher of the Year/Author: Molder of Dreams/Frequent Focus on the Family speaker.

Ordinary People,
ExtraOrdinary Marriages

Reclaiming God's Design for Oneness

Ordinary People, ExtraOrdinary Marriages

Reclaiming God's Design for Oneness

Brian A. Nystrom, MSW

Writer's Showcase
San Jose New York Lincoln Shanghai

Ordinary People, ExtraOrdinary Marriages
Reclaiming God's Design for Oneness

All Rights Reserved © 2001 by Brian A. Nystrom, MSW

No part of this book may be reproduced or transmitted in
any form or by any means, graphic, electronic, or mechanical,
including photocopying, recording, taping, or by any
information storage retrieval system, without the
permission in writing from the publisher.

Writer's Showcase
an imprint of iUniverse.com, Inc.

For information address:
iUniverse.com, Inc.
5220 S 16th, Ste. 200
Lincoln, NE 68512
www.iuniverse.com

Unless otherwise indicated in the text, Scripture references are from
The Holy Bible, New International Version, copyright © 1973, 1978, 1984 by
International Bible Society, inclusive version, 1995, 1996. Other versions used
are the New American Standard Bible (NASB) New International Version
Inclusive Language Edition(NIVI) and
the King James Version (KJV).

"The Lockhorns" cartoons are used by permission of King Features Syndicate.

ISBN: 0-595-15885-4

Printed in the United States of America

Contents

Preface

We are all ordinary people, but we don't have to settle for ordinary marriages. By challenging your thinking, this book will help to change how you view yourself, your spouse, and marriage itself. This book will help you on your marriage journey toward reclaiming God's original design for oneness in your marriage.

I don't want to give the impression that you can have or should expect a perfect marriage, because none of us will ever have a perfect marriage. We cannot expect one—because of our sinful natures, we are not capable of relating perfectly to one another. There will always be problems in our marriages. I have seen Christians feel like failures, personally and spiritually, because they could not live up to their own expectations for a perfect marriage. I think it is necessary to reframe our perspectives on marriage along with our expectations, and this book will try to help you do that. It will offer ways for you to apply your individuality and your Christianity in your most important human relationship: your marriage.

One of the many reasons for the writing of this book is because I believe marriages are an important stabilizing force in society. I believe that the family is the most powerful unit in society, and when the family unit crumbles, everything else does, too. God designed Adam and Eve as the first couple. The husband-wife partnership is the original, divine pattern, which is centered and stabilized by God. A major purpose of this book is to help two-parent families stay together and flourish, so that their marriages continue to stabilize society through their children, their neighborhoods, and their communities.

Finally, this book was written for my children and their children and your children and your children's children. As parents, one of our primary roles is to teach our children how to live and thrive. As our society shifts more and more toward secularization, Christian patterns of living will become more diluted, or perhaps they will be lost. We need to know the basis for what we do and how we operate. So do our children and grandchildren. I hope this book will help you as you build your knowledge and understanding of your Christian life and transmit that to your families.

This book is organized into three sections. The first section, chapters 1 through 5, introduces a number of influences that significantly affect your marriage. We'll examine these so that you are able to recognize them within your life and your marriage. These influences, and the ways we can change them, give us the tools to improve our marriages. In the second section, chapter 6, you'll be introduced to a partnership model of marriage from Genesis 1–2. The original creation was contaminated by sin, but we can reclaim God's design for our own marriages. In the final section, chapters 7 through 9, we'll examine ways of creating basic changes in your marriage, and we'll also look at how to strengthen a partnership marriage.

My prayer is that you will learn from this book on many levels and that you and your marriage will benefit from it.

Acknowledgements

By heartfelt thanks to the many who have helped in the formation of this project including: Alvera Mickelsen for unselfishly reading the manuscript several times and giving me honest feedback; Dr. Joy Elasky Fleming and Rev Bruce Fleming for their critical analysis of chapter 6 using the original Hebrew and Greek as a reference point; Jack Hinrichs, M.A., Tom Graske, L.P., Dr. Marcus Bachmann, Dr. Paul Warner, Dr. Lanny Law, Guy Doud, and Loren Fritzie, M.A. for their feedback on the concepts of the book; Linda Triemstra of Gold Leaf Editorial Services during the final draft; Jeanne and Bill Fudge for graciously allowing me to use their Lake Hubert retreat during the first writing; and Molly, Andy, Peter and Joey Nystrom for prompting the project by asking, "When will the book be ready?"

A deep bow of respect to all of the clients who shared their stories with me as we worked together to strengthen your marriages. You are courageous for sharing yourselves and making positive changes in your lives and marriages.

Finally, thanks to Mary Ann—my life partner who has been patient, honest and supportive to me over the years. We are partners in marriage till death do us part. Thank you Mary Ann for the countless hours we have spent discussing the concepts of the book and in your editing of the manuscript. I love you forever!

Chapter 1

Increasing Energy in Your Marriage

Marriage is the chief cause of divorce.

- Groucho Marx

If I had given as much to marriage as I gave to the *Tonight Show,* I'd probably have a hell of a marriage. But the fact is I haven't given that, and there you have the simple reason for the failure of my marriages. I put the *energy* into the show.

- Johnny Carson

Whether we are thinking about our needs as human beings or the world we live in, energy is required for everything we do. Everything from our bodies to our homes to our marriages requires the constant input of energy to maintain and improve them, or they will deteriorate.

Common wisdom says many marriages start out well, but they soon lose their magic. We even have a cliché for it: we say the honeymoon is over. As with many complicated subjects, there is more than one layer to this problem. On the most visible layer, the partners in these unions have stopped putting the same high levels of energy into the relationship as they did when they were first married. If we look deeper, we'll see that the relationship is changing, and the partners don't recognize it. They don't see

1

the change because none of us are born knowing how to stay married. We have to learn to stay married.

One of the main concepts we will explore in this book is how to reverse the deterioration or disorder that results from a lack of the loving energy that binds a husband and wife together. For the purpose of this book, we will coin the phrase *marital entropy* and define it as "the amount of disorder in a marriage." At any given time, every marriage has a certain amount of entropy in it. A marriage left on its own, with no energy or effort put into it, will eventually die. This is the ultimate form of marital entropy.

Any effort to improve a marriage requires that the husband and wife examine the sources and causes of entropy in their marriage. I will call these sources and causes entropy increasers. These are the actions, attitudes, or situations that increase the level of entropy in marriage. High levels of entropy do not give a satisfying feeling to the marriage, because the relationship is disordered. A husband and wife will feel more detached and disconnected from each other when there are higher levels of entropy in their marriage than when their relationship is more ordered.

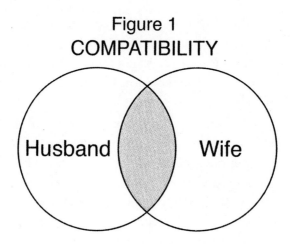

Figure 1
COMPATIBILITY

Husband   Wife

When I explain this concept in marriage counseling sessions, couples quickly understand it. They recognize the feeling! As entropy levels increase, it's as if each person is spinning off into his or her own orbit. Spouses begin to spend time away from their partners, develop independent interests, gravitate toward friends, work, or church, or possibly begin an extramarital affair.

In the courting and early marriage periods, most couples spend a great deal of time and energy getting to know and trying to understand each other. They have a high degree of compatibility (see fig. 1). These would include such things as common activities, common interests, time spent together, meaningful communication, or shared religious beliefs. Yet even though they are married, each spouse has his or her unique individuality and spends time doing things separately.

As the entropy levels rise, the relationship shifts (see fig. 2). For many couples, this shift toward entropy is a gradual process, taking place over varying lengths of time. In other cases one spouse may be oblivious to the entropy, thinking that everything is fine. The other spouse may feel trapped in a relationship he or she feels is characterized by anger, resentment, and despair.

Figure 2
ENTROPY

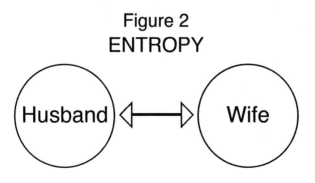

Retreat and Resentment: John and Sally

During Sally's first appointment, she revealed that John had suddenly left after twenty-five years of marriage. Although she saw no warning signals, one morning she woke up alone. John had abruptly moved out. In a separate interview John revealed that for all those years he felt Sally had not met his needs, had never really understood him, and had never tried to understand him. Over the years, these issues had developed into a deep resentment, even hatred, toward Sally.

John and Sally were both devout Christians who had a strong faith in Christ. John knew that leaving was not right, yet his resentment was so deep he could no longer tolerate being around Sally. Even loneliness was better than living with her, he told himself.

For her part, Sally desperately wanted to do whatever it would take to get John back, but over the years her negative traits, such as her unwillingness to look at herself, her defensiveness, and her habit of always blaming John had catalyzed the entropy in their marriage. John retreated into himself, his work, and his friends. This sort of retreat is also an entropy increaser. Early in their marriage, John had been unwilling to confront Sally to create honesty and authenticity in their relationship, and he no longer thought the relationship was worth the work to save it. Sally's high level of defensiveness prevented her from seeing John drift away. He left and never came back.

Family Influences: Cindy and Steve

During their courtship, Steve thought Cindy was attractive, practical, and nice. He decided she would be a good mate and proposed to her. For her part, Cindy thought Steve was handsome, communicated with her, and arranged romantic activities. He'd make an excellent husband, she decided, and she married him.

The honeymoon was a fantasy, but when they came home, Steve coldly and firmly announced that the fun was over—now they were married. Fifteen years later, after many conflicts and fights, Cindy and Steve finally came to see me.

Steve's upbringing was a major source of his personal entropy. Like most of us, he had learned how to be married by watching his parents in action. They had both worked long, hard hours throughout Steve's childhood. He recalled that his parents rarely laughed or seemed to have fun, and he had no memories of them socializing or recreating as a couple or with others.

Steve's parents had instilled in him a strong work ethic, and he was also taught frugality. Work and survival were the keys to life. During his fifteen years of marriage to Cindy, the beliefs that he had gained from his parents' example began to play themselves out. Steve worked long, hard hours at his business. Years went by between recreational activities and dates in his marriage. He constantly criticized Cindy for her spending habits. Cindy's resentment built over the years, and she found other outlets in her friends, her children, and her church activities. She began to find herself enjoying Steve's absences from home and resenting it when he would return. At times she even found herself wishing that Steve would die.

Through persistent confrontation Steve began to realize his contributions to the entropy in their marriage. Cindy also had to deal with her entropy increasers—including strong resentment, strong independence from Steve as a result of their lack of joint decision making, and spending major amounts of time away from home with friends and church activities. She had allowed herself to use her children to fill her emotional needs as a result of being emotionally starved by Steve.

Personal Satisfaction: Frank and Betty

Frank worked at an outdoor job doing manual labor, and he was exhausted when he came home. When he was in his twenties it was easy, but now he was in his mid-forties, and he felt his age. His routine was to come home after work, turn on the television, and sink into his comfortable chair with the newspaper. He worked hard and told himself that he deserved this treat, but his wife, Betty, had come to resent this habit. She had been providing daycare in their home all day, and she was emotionally and physically exhausted by 5 p.m. By early evening, she wanted to spend time with another adult, to talk, ventilate, and unload.

By treating himself to the television and newspaper, Frank effectively avoided meaningful interaction with Betty. Frank believed that everything was all right in his marriage, because this is what he had seen in his own family. He reasoned, "I've worked hard all day. I deserve to relax. We have a nice home and food on the table. Everything is fine." Betty told herself, "If he loved me he would give me some attention. He cares more about himself and that TV than he cares about me."

The entropy levels in Frank and Betty's marriage were increasing, while their marriage bonds were deteriorating. Every day weakened their relationship. Betty found satisfying companionship with her girlfriends and began to catch herself daydreaming about other men. She also found herself getting more and more depressed, and she began regularly using alcohol to make herself feel better.

Putting Energy into Marriage

John and Sally, Steve and Cindy, and Betty and Frank are typical of many couples coming for help. The great majority profess a Christian faith with varying degrees of intensity and church involvement. They are well-meaning people who care about their families and have a strong work ethic. However, their faith and their good intentions cannot prevent the entropy that touches every marriage. The list of problems married couples face is almost limitless, and all couples, Christian or not, face problems. All couples have some degree of entropy in their marriages.

Look again at the concept of entropy. Putting energy into marriage brings about increased compatibility. Failing to put energy into the system catalyzes entropy, causing deterioration of the marriage. The quote from Johnny Carson sums it up: Johnny put all of his energy into his work; his career thrived, while his marriages starved from entropy.

In my own marriage, I must be constantly vigilant to the entropy factors that I contribute, such as work, how I treat the children, or negative thinking that leads to the wrong conclusions. Unless factors such as these are dealt with successfully, my entropy increasers will push my wife, Mary Ann, away from me.

You might say, "Entropy? I've got enough to deal with." My reply to you is that entropy will build to a level of crisis that could damage or destroy your marriage. Why not take the time and energy to begin to analyze the entropy in your marriage? Then you can begin to make your marriage all that God intended it to be.

Questions for You and Your Spouse to Answer and Discuss

- How would you describe the entropy in your marriage?
- When did high entropy levels become a problem?
- What factors contributed to the entropy?

- How have beliefs of your family influenced the entropy?
- How does your self talk (your thoughts and internal reactions) influence the entropy?
- Write down specific areas to discuss with your spouse.
- Set an appointment with your spouse to discuss these areas.
- Look at the entropy trend in your marriage by rating the following periods in your relationship. Mark each continuum line with an *x* to show your entropy level at that time. What does your analysis show you?

Entropy_____Compatibility

Premarriage _____

Wedding _____

Five Years of Marriage _____

Fifteen Years of Marriage _____

Twenty Years of Marriage _____

Thirty Years of Marriage _____

Forty Years of Marriage _____

Chapter opening quote from Johnny Carson, *Time,* June 26, 1989, 6.

Chapter 2

How Our Families Influence
Our Marriages

A father tries to teach his sons or daughters to become all the things he wasn't, but most often you become everything he was.

- August Wilson, *Fences*

The environmental model of behavior says that as we grow from children to adults, each of us builds a unique set of life experiences. We develop our own values and rituals based on things that have happened to us or were taught to us by our parents, our extended families, or other influential people—what psychologists call birth families or families of origin, and what we will call families or upbringing. Many parts of us have been shaped or influenced by our upbringing, although I do believe genetics plays a part in who we are. Our political views, religious beliefs, and attitudes about other people have been influenced by our families.

It is also true that experiences that didn't happen or things that we didn't get will strongly influence us. For example, if a child has rarely been told "I love you" by his or her parents, the child will grow up feeling unlovable, with a sense of inadequacy. As an adult, he or she may have a

9

strong desire for acceptance from others. This person may use substances, such as drugs, alcohol, cigarettes, or food, or develop shielding habits, such as sex, work, or living on the edge, as a way to numb the pain from this perceived lack of acceptance. The adult might think, "If I don't feel my feelings, then I won't feel anything. If I don't feel anything, then I don't have a problem." It eventually becomes difficult to recognize our own feelings. Predictably, this makes it difficult to understand our spouses and to empathize with their issues and problems.

If a child has been abused or abandoned, he or she often grows up as a survivor, unaccustomed to trusting anyone. The survivor finds it hard to be vulnerable and open with his or her thoughts or feelings because of fear of further rejection and/or abandonment. The survivor may not even be able to trust his or her spouse—the same person the survivor just promised to cherish for a lifetime.

The child who was discouraged or invalidated by his or her parents will also have a sense of inadequacy as an adult. Instead of being willing to trust his or her own inner sense of values, the adult will look for validation externally. When one spouse consciously or unconsciously uses the other spouse to meet unfilled needs from his or her childhood, and uses unhealthy methods to achieve that fulfillment, the relationship descends into marital codependence.

In chapter 1 we saw how the values from Steve's and Frank's families contributed to entropy in their marriages. In this chapter we'll look at some other couples to see how their family influences contributed to entropy in their marriages.

Family Celebrations: Jim and Sharon

Jim's behaviors and attitudes had been deeply influenced by his upbringing. His parents and grandparents had given him a strong work ethic. His parents toiled from dawn to dusk every day to eke out a living. Their hard work left them little time for energy for nurturing activities, expressions of affection, or terms of endearment. They were too busy and too tired to nurture him as a child; he could not ever recall hearing his mother tell him "I love you." Therefore, he never learned the art of nurturing, and he never learned to feel accepted. Jim copied the only example he had—his parents'.

One example of the differences between Jim and Sharon could be seen in how they responded to their children's birthdays. Sharon loved to make birthdays special. She would decorate the house, make a cake, and invite neighbor children for a party. Jim's response was irritation; he considered birthday parties a waste of time and money. He invalidated his wife's actions and opinions with his put-downs.

Jim could not recall his mother ever having a birthday celebration for him as a boy. This was part of his parents' teaching about not spending time or money on impractical things. So the message that Jim received was that celebrating birthdays, specifically his own birthday, was impractical and unnecessary. Therefore he thought, "I must be impractical and unnecessary."

Jim had learned well how to be a practical spender and that celebrations of any kind were impractical. Therefore, he resented what he considered to be his wife's wasteful and impractical birthday celebrations for their children. Sharon, however, had grown up in a family in which her mother had shown special consideration for birthdays, even though the family was poor. Sharon brought this different belief into her marriage, and this difference caused Jim and Sharon to clash at every birthday celebration.

As we counseled, however, Jim told me more about his chronic marriage problems, his depression, and his feelings of inadequacy.

Lack of Acceptance: Jim and Sharon

Because his parents were too busy and too tired to spend much time with him, Jim never learned the art of nurturing, and he never learned to feel accepted. Jim's deep sense of inadequacy and lack of acceptance made him difficult to live with. Because of his low self-esteem he found it intolerable for his wife to question him. He would become irritated or throw a temper tantrum. He always had to be right, and this frequently caused him to invalidate his wife, because if he had to be right, everybody else had to be wrong. His poor treatment of her catalyzed Sharon's urge to distance herself from Jim even more, and it raised the entropy level in their marriage each time it happened.

This successful businessman never recognized his wife's compliments or saw how she was serving him. Whatever she did was never enough. He had a voracious appetite for love and acceptance and never believed that Sharon loved him enough.

This became a self-fulfilling prophecy: she couldn't possibly love him enough, because he always wanted more. Jim was certain nobody could love someone as wretched and defective as he was. Remember, Jim had these distorted beliefs about himself as a result of his upbringing. Because he felt rejected and abandoned by Sharon, he pulled away from her emotionally. Jim had learned this technique well in his childhood, and he was an expert at insulating himself from emotional hurt. He promised himself that nobody would hurt him again.

Since Jim believed he couldn't get love and acceptance from his wife, he looked elsewhere. He constantly sought the approval and acceptance of those around him. He was outgoing and gregarious. He always puzzled out subtle ways to make the other person feel important. Being extremely sensitive, he was an expert at reading people and knew what to do to make them feel special and important. As they felt important, they reciprocated the kindness and affirmation he had given them. This filled his unmet needs for love and acceptance.

Jim became addicted to getting acceptance from others. It felt so good, it was immediately gratifying, and it was so easy to do. The more of a high it became to Jim, the more of a threat it became to Sharon. She grew jealous and insecure watching her husband constantly maneuvering for acceptance and affirmation from other people, especially since he didn't make the same efforts with her. It particularly bothered her to see him seeking the acceptance of other women. Her jealousy and anger turned into a deep-seated hurt and resentment. This became another entropy increaser, driving the couple further apart.

Throughout his married life Jim rarely told Sharon that he loved her; he rarely showed her caring, sensitive affection or used terms of endearment when he spoke to her. His intentions were good, but when he tried to show his love, it came out the wrong way. The patterns he learned in his family pushed Sharon away. This was the opposite effect that Jim had wanted. He really wanted to be close to her but didn't know how to make that happen. His lack of knowing had created a chain of entropy increasers. Rather than being certain that he deserved to be loved, Jim felt that he was defective and unlovable, inadequate and incomplete. The emotional neglect and abandonment were too powerful for Jim to handle alone.

At this point Jim would have benefited from counseling to help him sort out these issues from his past and realize that Sharon was not responsible for making him whole and meeting all his needs. However, his pride and embarrassment made him unable to seek help.

Breaking the Cycle of Pain

Let me pause for a moment to say that I believe many people reading this can relate to Jim's pain. Many parents have emotionally neglected their children. Even worse, some parents abuse their children physically or sexually. Nonetheless, most parents do try to do the best they can with what they have and what they know. They were the result of their own upbringing, and they brought their experiences into their marriages; consequently, they passed those on to their children. Does that make it okay? No. But it eases some of the pain to know that in the overwhelming number of cases such treatment was unintentional. Some readers have suffered great pain from your families. The pain was and remains real. I want to validate that to you. The pain and the unresolved issues need to be dealt with eventually, because you must heal these wounds to reduce the chance of their becoming entropy increasers in your own marriage and family. You do not want your anger, hurt, resentment, or mistrust spilling into your marriage and family. We each have a responsibility to end the cycle of pain.

Even family counseling professionals experience these problems. For example, due to many unmet needs in my own childhood I transferred a strong need for approval and acceptance onto Mary Ann. I needed her to fill me on the inside with affirmations and admiration, and this put an undue burden on her. Mary Ann attempted to meet my needs, but due to my own inadequacies I was unable to fully recognize her efforts. My pleas for more only created more entropy and frustration and pushed her away. Ultimately I realized that she could not be expected to meet all my needs.

The hard part of family of origin issues is that they are so subtle and pervasive that we seldom know they are there unless we look for them. These are the assumptions on which we build our lives. We tend to assume that everyone else shares these beliefs, and we can be astonished to discover that they do not. Consider your first Christmas with your spouse.

Did his or her family celebrate this holiday the same way yours did? Did they invite more people, or fewer, or did they serve different traditional foods? Did their way of celebrating feel foreign, or perhaps unsatisfying? Was the event stressful? If so, it was probably because you had assumed that your way of celebrating, the way you learned from your family, was the right way. Of course, there are many ways to celebrate the birth of Christ, and it really doesn't matter whether you eat potluck or stuffed goose. But it may not feel right until you get used to it.

The negative issues that you bring into your marriage from your family will catalyze entropy. This transference of some beliefs from childhood to adulthood is common to everyone. The key is identifying those issues that cause entropy. Once we are aware of the existence of family issues and know how to look for them, we need to remain open to the idea that we may find more of them in the future. We may have insights that lead us to see entropy increasers in something we didn't see yesterday. Be ready for this. Life is fluid, dynamic, and always changing. Ask God to help you be aware of issues from your past that might be serving as entropy increasers in your marriage now.

Shame and Not Owning a Problem

The habit of not owning a problem goes back to Adam and Eve. We can draw several points from their act of defiance to God, the first human sin.

Prior to the fall Adam and Eve did not know about their nakedness (Genesis 3:10-11). In their state of innocence, they were free to be who they were. They were not trying to make themselves look good on the outside, because they didn't have to be afraid of showing who they really were. They had committed no sin, so they showed how it was. We, however, have sinned, so we do not want to show how it is. Instead we show what we think others want to see, in order to gain their acceptance. This is shame-based behavior.

Note that Adam blames Eve and God for his sin (Genesis 3:12). But Adam had a choice, as Eve did, and he chose to sin. This placed Adam in a shame state, and his shame caused him to blame Eve and God. He wanted to look good to God and avoid responsibility for his choice. He blamed Eve and God, but as adults we need to accept responsibility for our own actions and attitudes.

Adam and Eve hid from God, just as we hide our problems from others, including our spouses and children. It is dysfunctional to keep information about ourselves from our spouses, because we are not entitled to secrecy within a marriage. Secrecy and other shame-based behaviors stimulate entropy. Marriage partners must constantly work at being honest and transparent with each other within the relationship. This kind of communication doesn't always come naturally, however, and in later chapters we will look at how to communicate honestly and transparently without destroying the other person. Being honest and transparent is much easier when we know how to identify the family of origin issues that will influence our reactions to volatile situations.

Some Christians fall into the trap of wanting things to look better than they truly are. Like many organized groups that foster a sense of belonging, churches can inadvertently create an environment in which members who are hurting are afraid to be open about it, because of what others might think. Some people are afraid to lose that sense of belonging. Therefore, members may be influenced not to reveal more about themselves because of a fear of rejection from other members. This drives the shame-based person to withdraw and not discuss problems or hurts. The shame-based person will do everything possible to make things appear to be fine, even if they are not, in order to gain acceptance and approval. The idea of rejection is so unpleasant and distasteful that many people avoid being open and honest with others.

We hold inside our hurts, defects, arguments, problems, failures, pain, addictions, sins, marriage and family problems. We shield our problems from others. Most people go to great lengths to avoid rejection, as we'll see in the story of Ann and Mark. Since each of us values the good opinion of our spouses, it is easy to fall into this shielding mode within a marriage. Many people have a difficult time identifying and sharing their own problems, mistakes, or errors with their spouse. It exposes our vulnerability to acknowledge a negative, destructive, or sinful motive that only we know about.

Rejection, Shame, and Abandonment: Ann and Mark

Many people come into my office with multiple problems. A classic example of this was Ann, who was clinically depressed, had a severe obsessive-compulsive disorder, and had long-standing marriage problems. She quickly revealed a life characterized by deep rejection: from her parents during her childhood; from her husband, Mark; and from her friends. She described her marriage as 95 percent negative, filled with arguments, invalidations, or being ignored by Mark. He would come home from work and head for his chair or the couch and read or nap. In the evenings he would find ways to leave the house. Many times he could justify this as work-related, as he was a pastor.

Pastors are usually overworked and underpaid; they are on call twenty-four hours a day, seven days a week. It is difficult for them to set boundaries between their job responsibilities and their family responsibilities. The pastoral job itself can be a source of entropy, and therefore it must be constantly managed and checked to maintain a healthy balance. In the case of Ann and Mark, his pastoral position became a source of entropy that he used to insulate himself from his wife and children.

Ann's sense of rejection and abandonment, which was already strong, intensified as Mark pulled away from her. This fueled an even deeper rejection that she had experienced growing up.

Ann was reared in a middle-class family. Her father was a professional, and they attended church every Sunday. They conformed to every appropriate social value and did everything the way they were supposed to. But as is often the case, the family behaved very differently in private.

Ann's parents yelled at her and physically abused her. Her parents never allowed her to express her opinions, thoughts, or ideas; they had emotionally banished her. Ann was taught to go along to get along and to be quiet in order to stay out of trouble. She learned through experience that her thoughts and opinions were not valuable and that she was much better off keeping them to herself. No one was allowed to disagree with others, so Ann learned that she must not speak up if she didn't agree. Harmony was more important than agreement.

Because of these childhood teachings, Ann repressed her feelings and thoughts. Since she believed her contributions to be unworthy, she felt a deep rejection (see fig. 3). Over many years of this treatment, Ann came to believe there was something defective about her. The type of treatment she received fueled her sense of shame about herself and made her feel rejected, abandoned, unlovable, and unworthy. Yet she sorely wanted approval, as all of us do.

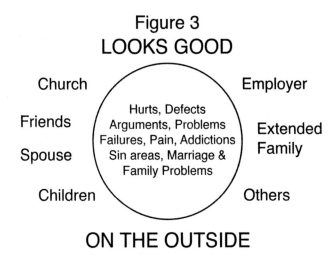

Figure 3
LOOKS GOOD

Church · Employer · Friends · Hurts, Defects, Arguments, Problems, Failures, Pain, Addictions, Sin areas, Marriage & Family Problems · Extended Family · Spouse · Children · Others

ON THE OUTSIDE

The treatment that Ann received from her parents had deepened her feelings of shame and her perception of lack of acceptance. When she married, Ann thought that things would change and that she would be able to communicate freely with her husband. She thought that she would be able to give him her opinions and interact with him intellectually in a beneficial way. But Mark grew up in a family that didn't discuss the personal things that affected them deeply, and therefore Mark had a difficult time expressing his innermost thoughts. His own feelings of being unlovable and unworthy led him to shame-based behavior. When Ann would ask him questions, he would react defensively; he would retreat emotionally and be silent. Many times he would mutter a caustic or condescending word under his breath, sometimes just loudly enough for Ann to hear. This caused Ann to feel hurt, fueling her old memories of rejection from her childhood.

This pattern of interaction had gone on for almost twenty years. Mark kept his feelings to himself to avoid a conflict with Ann, who interpreted his silence as abandonment. When Mark would share something with

Ann, she was no longer able to listen. This was especially true if he dis-agreed with her, because she had been taught that a marriage required per-fect harmony. She turned her feelings of abandonment into verbalized anger, and another conflict was born. This self-fulfilling prophecy merely convinced Mark to continue his dysfunctional approach to Ann. Likewise, Ann's entropy increaser was her inability to effectively convey to Mark her deep rejection and hurt. Instead, her pent-up feelings came out to Mark as anger and hostility. For his part, Mark was unable to risk Ann's anger, because it would deepen his childhood feelings of unworthiness. They drove each other away (see fig. 4).

Figure 4
ENTROPY CATALYSTS

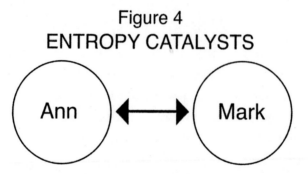

While each of us must choose the right time to deal with our own issues, in this case both spouses endured great suffering as a result of not knowing what the issues were. The key is that you do not have to wait a long time to deal with your family issues. You can begin to identify them now and determine how they have been transferred into your marriage.

Questions for You and Your Spouse to Answer and Discuss

- What did you learn in your family about marriage and family? How do these ideas transfer into your marriage? (Examples would include communication, levels of affection, sex, types and frequency of recreation, discipline of children, conflict resolution, money, or religion.)
- Have any of these issues increased entropy in your marriage? If so, how?
- Are members of your extended family currently enforcing any dysfunctional patterns? If so, what are those patterns?
- Are there areas in which you need to let go of old issues or patterns from your family (present or past)?
- Have you ever been stuck in a certain pattern of marital behavior to find out that it was related to your family? Be specific.
- List messages that you picked up while you were growing up that have been transferred into marriage on the left side. Then list a more balanced belief statement on the right side.

Family of Origin Marital Mistaken Misbelief   Balanced Belief

Chapter opening quote is from *Corporate Report Minnesota,* October 1992, 85.

Chapter 3

The Ins and Outs of Self Talk

As a man thinks, so he is.
- Proverbs 23:7 (paraphrased from KJV)

I am always with myself, and it is I who am my own tormentor.
- Leo Tolstoy

Deep down in his heart no man much respects himself.
- Mark Twain

We have seen that our beliefs and assumptions follow us from childhood into our married lives, where they can become entropy increasers. Another major source of entropy can be our self talk, which is the continuously running commentary we have in our thoughts. Self talk is about our lives, our interpretation of our surroundings, input from our senses, thoughts, ideas, opinions, fantasies, wants, needs, knowledge, and facts. Even while we sleep, our minds are active. We self talk at the same time we engage another person in conversation. This fascinating and powerful process that influences everything we do.

Nothing happens to us that we don't comment on internally; even little thoughts such as "I don't like what's happening now" or "I'm uncomfortable" or "I'm bored—how can I slip out of here?" are self talk. Researchers tell us that in the average conversation, individuals talk at a rate of about 150 to 200 words per minute. However, self talk can run at a rate of 1,300 words per minute.[1] The important thing to realize is that instances of self talk, or cognitions, occur at precisely the same time as our external conversations. Our minds can run much faster than our mouths and ears can. These internal messages add flavor and texture to what is happening externally, but they're so subtle that we may not realize that it is we who are adding the meanings.

The connection between self talk and marriage is complicated, and some counselors try to improve marriages by taking only a behavioral approach. There is some value in this perspective, and some biblical support for it also: Jesus said, "However you want people to treat you, so treat them" (Matthew 7:12, NASB). But this behavioral perspective can lead to further resentment and entropy. For example, there was a time in my career as a marriage and family therapist when I would try to get couples to meet each other's needs. I would ask that they do things together, such as spend time together or have sex. Some couples responded well to this method, but many did not. As a matter of fact, this prescription became an entropy increaser for many couples. This was a puzzle for me. They were supposed to improve, but they didn't. I became very aware that lasting behavioral changes have to be based on real changes in our thinking patterns. Part of this change in our thinking patterns depends on learning about how our self talk affects us.

---

1. "A Key to Change—Your Self Talk Can Build You Up or Tear You Down," *Christian Psychology* (fall 1989): 8-10. There are many excellent Christian and secular books on self talk.

For example, it became clear to me that during a session with Frank and Sandy that merely meeting needs was not enough. Frank had done everything right for Sandy for the past six months. He had met her needs, listened to her, worked hard at being a good dad, and said no to some of his work demands in order to spend time at home. Frank got an A on his homework assignments. He shared this in a session and admitted he found himself feeling anger and resentment toward Sandy. Frank burst out, "I've met all your needs these past six months and done everything right, but you still won't give me sex!" Sandy's response was, "So all of these behaviors were only meant to get me into bed!" This realization increased her distrust in Frank's motives and caused her to doubt the authenticity of his actions over the past six months. And, as we talked through this issue, Frank finally agreed with her assessment.

Frank, like many of us, had fallen into the performance orientation or works model of life that says, "If I try hard enough, I'll get what I want." But changing a behavior, without an accompanying change of thinking, will have short-lived results. This is why Frank had a problem—he changed his behaviors but not his accompanying thought patterns. He eventually tired of artificially changing behaviors, especially since it wasn't buying him the response he wanted from Sandy. Behavioral methods alone usually will not reduce entropy in a marriage. The marriage is reduced to two people who are only meeting needs and doing tasks, but it misses a deeper relational level.

True change starts with changing or restructuring our thoughts or thought patterns, a process known as cognitive restructuring. Restructuring your thoughts or beliefs to another perspective will produce a change in emotion and behavior. This is referred to as the cognitive-behavioral model. The consequence of changing beliefs or thoughts is an accompanying change in emotion and behavior.

Self talk affects marriages because self talk affects feelings, emotions, and behaviors. All of our feeling, emotions, and behaviors are driven by all of these things we are continually telling ourselves. Our thoughts produce our feelings and emotions, and our thoughts strongly influence our actions and behaviors. Our feelings, emotions, and behaviors are the direct results of our thoughts (see fig. 5). No one else is responsible for them—we are.

Figure 5

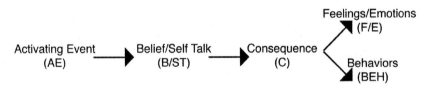

Some other principles of self talk are:
- Self talk produces our feelings and emotions.
- Self talk influences our behaviors.
- Parts of our self talk are irrational, distorted, or negative.
- Irrational, distorted, or negative thought patterns will produce unnecessary negative emotions and behaviors.
- Influence from our family and our religious and cultural backgrounds have shaped some of the beliefs that make up our self talk.

Demand words, such as "must," "always," "should," or "ought to," are likely to create a demand on another person or on ourselves in our self talk. For example, Frank said to himself, "Sandy *will* give me more sex." This is a classic example of a demand in our self talk. When the demand is not met, as in Frank's case, we tend to get angry. We all make demands in our self talk, and many times it's difficult to pinpoint them.

It's important to try to shift our demands or desires in our self talk. For example, Frank could shift from "Sandy *will*" to "Sandy *might* give me more sex." What seems to be subtle is a major change. It will help Frank deal with his demand in his self talk by downgrading an unspoken ultimatum to a desire that may or may not be met. Changing from a demand to a desire will reduce entropy levels as well as decrease Frank's anger and resentment. It won't obliterate all negative emotions, but it will significantly reduce negative emotions in a given situation.

Identifying Irrational Thoughts

Most people who read or hear about self talk have no problem recognizing it. It's hard to ignore something that you do constantly. The hard part for most people is how to tell when a given thought is irrational, negative, or distorted. Since we've lived with these thoughts all of our lives, it's hard to tell which are reasonable or rational and which are unreasonable or irrational. This immediately shows us the difficulty in dealing objectively with our own thoughts.

There are several avenues for us to take to be able to identify our negative thoughts. The first is general awareness that we sometimes have thought patterns that are distorted. None of us is perfect, and we all fall prey to this. Our sinful nature and dysfunctional family of origin influences will cause distorted beliefs and cognitions. What follows are fifteen types of distorted thinking.[2]

---

2. Albert Ellis is credited with founding Rational-Emotive Therapy (R.E.T.) and Aaron Beck with cognitive therapy. Of course, Christian Scripture is the true foundation for self talk and its powerful influence(e.g., Proverbs 23:7, quoted at the beginning of the chapter).

We *filter* information when we magnify the negative details while minimizing the positive aspects of a situation.

We practice *polarized thinking* when we think things are black and white, good or bad. We may think we have to be perfect or we're failures. There is no middle ground.

Overgeneralization occurs when we come to a general conclusion based on a single incident or piece of information. If something bad happens we expect it to happen over and over again.

We presume to *mind read* other people when we assume we can tell what people are feeling and why they act the way they do. In particular, we may think we are able to divine how people are feeling about us.

We *catastrophize* when we continually expect disaster. We may take a small problem and start to magnify it. What if tragedy strikes? What if the worst happens?

We *personalize* our thinking by believing that everything people do or say is some kind of reaction to us. We also compare ourselves with others, trying to determine who's smarter, better looking, and so forth.

We have *control fallacies.* If we feel externally controlled, we see ourselves as helpless victims of fate. On the other end of the spectrum, that fallacy of internal control tells us that we are responsible for the pain and happiness of everyone around us.

The *fallacy of fairness* leads us to feel resentful because we think we know what's fair, but other people won't agree with us.

Blaming occurs when we hold other people responsible for our pain, or perhaps we take the other tack and blame ourselves for every problem or reversal.

Shoulds provide us with a list of ironclad rules about how we and everyone else should act. People who break the rules anger us, and we feel guilty if we violate the rules.

Emotional reasoning develops when we believe that what we feel must automatically be true. If we feel stupid and boring, then we must *be* stupid and boring.

In the *fallacy of change,* we expect that other people will change to suit us if we just pressure or cajole them enough. We need to change people because our hopes for happiness seem to depend entirely on them.

If we must *continually be right,* then we are always on trial to prove that our opinions and actions are correct. Being wrong is unthinkable, and we will go to any length to demonstrate how right we are.

If we hold to the *heaven's reward fallacy,* we expect all our sacrifice and self-denial to pay off, as if there were someone keeping score. We feel bitter when the reward doesn't come.

A second way to identify negative or distorted thought patterns is by checking them out with a spouse or another person. Sometimes it's hard to take feedback, especially on something as intimate as our thoughts, but try to be open to this. Pray for the strength to try, because awareness and knowledge are the first steps to changing any distorted thoughts.

Third, use the following questions as a worksheet to become aware of your thought patterns and ensuing emotions and behaviors. Try to be honest and authentic. Don't try to fool yourself—be real!

Remember that an activating event leads to self talk, and self talk leads to consequences, either in feelings and emotions or in behaviors.

Questions to ask:

What was the activating event (situation or circumstance)?

What specific self statements did you make to yourself about the situation?

What feelings and emotions were generated as a result of these self statements?

How did you behave at that point? What were your actions and words?

This exercise works best if we can share the results with a spouse or a friend. Do this several times. Look for patterns or connections between thoughts and emotions. This method is effective in addressing entropy increasers such as emotional discomfort or negative behaviors. It works when analyzing and dealing with emotions such as anger, resentment, or rejection; it also works when you are on the receiving end of such behaviors as silence, yelling, or physical abuse. The trick is to think the situation through carefully and trace what was said or done, what self talk was generated, and what emotions and behaviors resulted. This isn't an easy skill to learn, but we must face these entropy increasers when we meet them.

Disputation

Once negative thoughts are identified, the next part of the process is learning how to dispute negative self talk. The act of disputation will counter irrational thoughts, a process that over time will yield a more balanced and truthful perception in any given situation. This is also a difficult process to learn, but when we master it, it allows us to take control of the entropy increasers that result from our own behavior. The Serenity Prayer may remind you to identify which things you can control and which you can't:

Lord, grant me the serenity to accept the things I cannot change, courage to change the things I can, and the wisdom to know the difference.

The process is this: we identify negative or irrational thoughts, dispute those thoughts, and come to balance and truth in our thoughts (see fig. 6).

Figure 6
The Process Looks Like This:

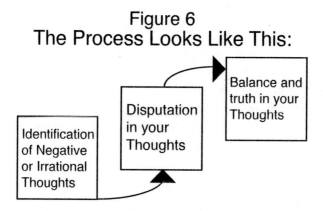

These methods will help you to develop your skill in reducing irrational thinking: Choose one of the situations in which you have identified negative thinking. Identify all of the self statements from the situation that are distorted, negative, or irrational. In what way could you change the negative statements into one that is more balanced and truthful?

The list that follows gives several examples of possible negative thoughts and a restatement that represents the result of disputing the negative thought.

I am stupid.
I am fairly intelligent. I'm rearing children and holding a job.

I am ugly.

My husband finds me attractive. My negative thoughts are from a poor self-image. I'm made in God's image and therefore I have great value.

I don't know the Bible as well as others do.
I may not have memorized great portions of the Bible, but I know the basics. Besides, God is more interested in my faithfulness, not my ability to memorize.

I don't pray well in public.
I'm more on the introverted side. God is not interested in fancy or melodramatic prayers but rather in what comes from my heart.

If we dispute each negative thought and replace it with a more balanced, truthful perspective, over time we begin to believe the truth more and more. This will ultimately lead to more confidence and boldness in our lives. This won't happen overnight; this process goes on over our lifetimes. But the more we can be aware of our irrational thought patterns and the more we dispute them, the more balance we will have in our thinking and in our lives. This balance will decrease the entropy in this area of our lives.

In the next chapter we will look at specific examples of how self talk can cause entropy in marriage.

Homework for You and Your Spouse

You can do the following assignments alone or with your spouse to help you in identifying and disputing your negative thoughts.

For one day, list all the distorted, negative, or irrational self statements that you make or are aware of.

Parallel each item in the left column with a more balanced, truthful statement based on Scripture, what others have told you, or what you know is really the truth.

Practice reviewing and telling yourself the truth (the statement in the right column) several times a day.

Ask God to help you imprint the truth in your mind.

When the distorted, negative, or irrational thought occurs, immediately dispute it with the truth.

Negative/Distorted/Irrational   Balance/Truth

1.   1.
2.   2.
3.   3.
4.   4.

Chapter 4

Self Talk and Communication in Your Marriage

Nature has given us one tongue but two ears, that we may hear from others twice as much as we speak.

- Epictetus

We have learned so far that every couple has some degree of entropy in their relationship. In chapter 2 we saw the impact of family beliefs and how those beliefs, messages, and unmet needs are transferred into marriage. We've also learned that self talk is the tool we use to change behaviors and feelings. Mental health professionals call this cognitive therapy and cognitive restructuring. A vast body of clinical research supports the cognitive approach for lasting emotional and behavioral change.

Now we need to examine how our self talk, with all of its various influences, increases entropy in our marriage. We've seen that we all have distorted, negative, or irrational threads in our self talk. Imagine for a moment what happens when we put together two individuals to be married and live together and interact frequently. What every couple gets is a communication pattern jumbled with distortions and assumptions and family issues. It's no wonder that successful marriages take a lot of work!

Couples face several problems when dealing with marital self talk or self talk in general.

First, many individuals, especially men, seem to be unaware of their self talk. Men typically have a hard time identifying their thoughts, let alone articulating them. I have found that with enough practice, such as with the assignments in chapter 3, men do get better at this.

Second, men have a tough time identifying their feelings. Comments like "I don't feel anything" or "I don't know my feelings" or "I don't know what a feeling is" are common among the male clients in my office. Again, I believe that with enough practice and encouragement, most men can improve in this area. In the very early years of our relationship Mary Ann had to give me multiple-choice questions to help me identify my feelings. I am living proof that men can change.

Third, self talk is intimate and personal to you. By its nature, it causes all of us to be somewhat self-absorbed in our thinking. You lose track of whether or not you've shared this or that detail with your spouse. You forget things momentarily, or your perspective changes. The solution is to try to come out of your self-absorption and share with your spouse.

Fourth, we may have learned family rules or messages that say "don't share things" or "if it's going to cause pain to the other person, don't do it." However, the more we keep our feelings inside, the more entropy will develop. Eventually things come out in a relationship, whether we want them to or not. Sometimes we fear rejection or conflict and therefore we don't want to share. Or we may have sinned and are too ashamed to share it. Holding things in will cause emotional, physical, and relationship problems. The truth is that we have to learn to deal with everything in a marriage relationship. There cannot be any secrets from your spouse.

Fifth, the Bible gives many references to our shame-based nature, and we've already looked at the story of Adam and Eve. This shows it is natural for us not to want to admit our faults, defects, flaws, or negative thoughts to our partners. It is much easier to keep them to ourselves. We all want to look good, and we are fearful of rejection and nonacceptance by others. Being honest can be uncomfortable or painful. Being honest about ourselves in our marriages tales a great deal of energy. Honest communication is one of the most effective weapons that we have against entropy in a marriage. Through Scripture, God encourages us to deal with each other with truth and honesty. Consider Ephesians 4:25 (NIVI): "Therefore each of you must put off falsehood and speak truthfully to your neighbor, for we are all members of one body."

I would hope that your spouse is your closest neighbor. Shame-based behaviors and keeping secrets are types of falsehood and deception we all exhibit at times—and deception and falsehood both increase entropy. In later chapters we will look at how to effectively communicate truth. We must recognize that truthful communication must also be accomplished with respect and love, because sometimes we can be honest in a cruel or sarcastic way that creates entropy. These issues need to be examined in every marriage.

The Need for Honesty: Vivian and Dick

The case of Vivian and Dick illustrates the need for complete honesty in a marriage. Dick traveled extensively on business. On his trips he had engaged in brief sexual encounters with various women, and he had kept theses encounters a secret for several years. Dick knew that what he had done was sinful. His affairs affected him the same way King David's guilt affected him. Dick was wasting away inside, consumed by guilt. He told himself, "If I tell Vivian about the affairs it will cause her immense pain and suffering. I can't hurt her. So I'll keep this to myself." Likewise, in Psalm 32:3-5 (NIVI), David wrote, "When I kept silent, my bones wasted away through my groaning all day long. For day and night your hand was heavy upon me; my strength was sapped as in the heat of summer. Then I acknowledged my sin to you and did not cover up my iniquity. I said, 'I will confess my transgressions to the LORD'—and you forgave the guilt of my sin."

Dick was tired of holding in his sin, so it took little convincing for him to confess to Vivian. His self talk was accurate in predicting that his confession would cause Vivian a lot of pain. She was devastated and emotionally raw for several months afterward. But through Dick's confession, he decided to be a better husband and began to deal with his issues. Vivian began to deal with her issues and gradually developed a graceful, forgiving attitude toward Dick. Dick's confession to Vivian ultimately brought them closer together than they had ever been in their twenty-five years of marriage. His honesty, painful as it was, decreased the entropy in their marriage. Honesty isn't easy—applying the principles in this book calls for great courage and maturity.

Self Talk: Ann and Mark Revisited

We met Ann and Mark earlier and examined how they struggled with family issues that were transferred into their marriage. Now we will look again at their relationship and apply everything we've learned so far.

We rejoin Mark and Ann as Mark returned home one evening. He walked through the front door, straight past Ann, without making eye contact or speaking. Their sensitivity levels were so high that merely being in her presence or seeing her irritated Mark. His self talk was racing, saying things such as "I can't stand being around her. Whatever I say won't be good enough. Why should I even try to discuss things? It only ends up in a fight."

Simultaneously, these thoughts produced feelings of anxiety, rejection, despair, inadequacy, and a churning stomach. The behaviors and physical reactions that were influenced by Mark's self talk included avoiding Ann or making no eye contact with her.

Mark's avoidance triggered Ann's self talk, which went something like this: "Here we go again. He'll never change. He really doesn't love me and never has. He's such a phony. He looks so good to everyone else, but with me and the kids he's a fake. If others really knew the truth…"

Ann's thoughts produced feelings of rejection, anger, abandonment, and rage. Her thoughts strongly influenced her behavioral reaction of yelling sarcastically at Mark, "Mark, talk to me—you never do—be a real husband instead of a fake!"

Ann's last comment became Mark's next activating event. Silently Mark would tell himself, "She really is b—. She's so screwed up. She'll never change. I resent her. If only I could, I'd divorce her."

These thoughts only produced more resentment, anger, and hurt. Mark wondered if he should defend himself or retreat. He decided to retreat. He also emotionally shut himself off from Ann. As silently as he had entered, Mark walked out of the room and away from Ann.

His physical and emotional retreat touched off Ann's self talk, which said, "He's a jerk. He doesn't put any effort into this marriage or family. Our marriage is a joke. I'm stuck."

Her feelings of resentment, rejection, and abandonment intensified. As Mark walked off, she expressed her feelings by yelling "Damn you!" at his retreating back.

Self Talk, Upbringing, and Communication

This interaction took place in less than a minute. Many marital interactions are brief. Note also that although Mark never said a word aloud, there were two complete sets of self talk that spoke volumes. Our self talk is constantly analyzing our environment, giving us feedback, interpreting events from our own perspectives, and editorializing life around us. Mark and Ann had been in this pattern or a long time. Did you notice the rapid, reactionary nature of their interactions? This is because the other person's comments, behaviors, body language, facial movements, tone of voice, volume, pitch, and nonreactions all can trigger the other person's self talk. One spouse doesn't need to speak a response for the other spouse to hear a response.

Simultaneously, our personalities, family issues, cumulative experiences, and composite experiences with our spouses are all mixing at the same moment. And all of this happens very rapidly, because our brains are so powerful.

Remember that Ann had been emotionally neglected and abused by her parents. Her opinions didn't matter, nor was she allowed to express them to her parents. What her father said and did were all that was important to her family. Her father could chastise her and walk away. Now her husband could walk through the front door without acknowledging her.

Deep within her some old tapes were playing, and these tapes were playing old tunes called rejection, abandonment, and lack of self-worth. Ann just wanted to be loved by Mark. "Is that so much to ask for?" she constantly wondered. Ann felt like Loretta Lockhorn did (**cartoon 1**).

THE LOCKHORNS

Ann's personality made her sensitive and rejection-oriented. She would find hurt in situations where there wasn't any. She perceived herself as being likely to be rejected, and therefore her self talk reflected that she thought others saw her this way, too. She would then read the perceived rejection into interpersonal or social interactions and tell herself that others were rejecting her. She did this with Mark many times. Often she would push situations with Mark to get what she thought was the truth out of him until he would react negatively to her. His negative reactions then became a self-fulfilling prophecy that he did not love her. Worse, she thought that this proved she was unlovable. This complicated dynamic resulted from a combination of pieces from her upbringing that were transferred into the marriage, along with pieces of Mark's upbringing.

Mark's actions of walking away and shutting down, both emotionally and verbally, triggered another family dynamic for Ann. She was accustomed to her father having absolute authority over her; she could never give a rebuttal or state another point of view to him. This left Ann feeling helpless with her father. As most of us would, she resented this helplessness. When Mark would walk away, her resentment and helplessness from her childhood were immediately transferred into her current situation. Mark, who thought he was dealing with a situation that had lasted twenty seconds, was dealing with something that had lasted for twenty years.

For his part, Mark had built up an emotional barrier to Ann over the years. This type of insulation was protection, he thought, from allowing Ann to hurt him. Mark's family allowed him to grow up in an independent, autonomous, and nonaccountable environment. He was not used to talking things out with anybody, certainly not with his wife. He was his own captain, and he considered himself reasonable and kind. He told himself that his wife was the one with the problem. If she could only see the root of her deep problems, he reasoned, then she would have the insight to change.

For Mark, a noncommuincative posture was normal and acceptable, just as it had been when he was growing up. He thought that if his wife required anything more than this, it must be the result of how demanding, neurotic, hysterical, and emotionally needy she was. Because he didn't think it was necessary, he never learned to share himself with his wife. The truth was he didn't know how to open up to her. He didn't even know the basics of communication, yet he counseled others in his ministry. Ann's negativity, which was partly born out of Mark's communication style, pushed him further and further away; his retreating pushed her away. They didn't have an argument, but the repercussions of their self talk were every bit as severe. Their marital interactions and self talk were entropy increasers. Their quick reactions toward each other created a reactionary, downward spiral that made it difficult to sort out the real issues (see fig.

7). This was especially true when their respective family issues were considered. In each instance, the behavior exhibited by one spouse was the activating event for the other spouse. Downward cycling is a result of unhealthy and dysfunctional communication patterns.

Figure 7
ENTROPY-PRODUCING INTERACTIONS

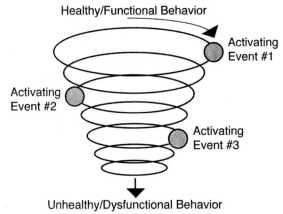

Since we all self talk, and parts of our self talk are irrational and distorted by sin and influences from our families, it follows that marital self talk problems are entropy increasers in all marriages. Self talk is universal and cuts across religious, racial, gender, and socioeconomic lines.

How to Restructure Thoughts

If the process of communication is not straightened out, it will deteriorate into severe entropy. But there are strategies and tools to correct this problem. Each one requires energy. For example, Mark might have disputed his thoughts: "At one time I did love Ann. Maybe I'm not listening to her. She does have other friends. If she's as bad as I'm trying to make her, then she wouldn't have any friends. I need to keep trying to work on our relationship. Not working on it only fuels entropy. I wonder how my upbringing has influenced me to be and react the way I do?"

Mark's preliminary restructuring of his thought will cause him to reshape how he views Ann and his own contribution to the problem. He will approach Ann less defensively and less resentfully than before. The new thoughts will allow him to make eye contact with Ann and greet her instead of ignoring her.

Ann might restructure her thoughts: "The two of us have been in a negative rut for so long. Both of us can change, but we don't know how. At one time he showed me his love. I know he's not very demonstrative with his feelings because of how he was reared. I know that I am very sensitive and rejection-oriented because that's how I was reared. I know because of this I read rejection into Mark's actions. I know he's not a phony. I know his ministry is real, and he tries to obey God. He's just very frustrated, like I am, and he feels stuck."

By restructuring her original, negative thoughts, Ann's more positive self talk will help prevent her from spiraling downward into greater entropy. This also will help her to resist yelling at Mark or being nasty to him.

Both spouses need to constantly evaluate their self statements and how they interpret and editorialize their environments.

Many times it is necessary to test our self talk by checking it with our spouses if we're not sure of what's happening or if we need clarification. For example, after Ann and Mark had been in therapy for a while, Ann had a nagging concern that she wanted to raise. She asked Mark, "I was telling myself that you have never loved me. Is that my negative self talk or is this true?" This gave Mark an opportunity to speak for himself instead of Ann mind reading what she thought he was thinking. Checking things out is good communication in marriage. But there can be many obstacles to communication, and we will examine them throughout this book. Again, checking things out with your spouse and the ongoing disputation of negative thoughts are both essential to reducing conflict and entropy.

Activating Events and Self Talk: Paul and Lisa

Paul is an executive at a large company, and he works long hours. His workaholic style causes him to project his work habits onto his wife. He thinks, "I work long hours. So should she." Lisa does work hard as a full-time mother with young children who constantly demand energy from her. In the situation we'll analyze, Paul is coming home late one night after working a typical twelve-hour day. The activating event, or trigger, is that Paul walks into the kitchen and sees dirty dishes in the sink. Tools from one of Lisa's do-it-yourself remodeling projects are strewn on the table.

Paul's self talk is this: "If she wouldn't do all of these projects, then she would have time to rear our children properly. The kids wouldn't be so spoiled and selfish if Lisa was firmer and wouldn't give in to their every whim. These projects are a waste of time and money and don't give us an adequate return on investment. Lisa's never satisfied with what she has. She always wants more. My simple lifestyle is the right one. She wants more and more. She's the problem. She's like my mother, who was never satisfied. Women gain, men lose..."

Paul feels anger, frustration, resentment, and sadness. As a result he says sarcastically "Well, I see the house is shipshape again tonight. You're home with the kids all day. Can't you at least keep the house clean?"

For Lisa, the activating event is Paul's sarcastic comment, and it provokes this self talk: "He doesn't love me. He doesn't understand me. I'd like to see him stay home all day with young children. Maybe I should go out and get a job just to show him I can do it."

She feels rejection, hurt, anger, and resentment, and therefore she lashes out at Paul, saying, "At least the children know what I look like. You're gone so much, they hardly know you!"

In the next part of their exchange, Paul's activating event is that Lisa lashed out at him, resulting in this self talk: "I work all day for her, and all she can do is yell at me. I hate her. All I want is love and respect! Lisa is a #$%!"

He feels deeper anger, frustration, resentment, and resignation, so he storms out of the room and slams the door. He doesn't speak to Lisa until the next day.

For Lisa, the next activating event is that Paul leaves the room, slams the door, and is silent. Her self talk is the same as before, only it is intensified, and she adds, "He repulses me. But maybe it's all me." She feels anger, resentment, abandonment, hurt, and confusion. In reaction she cries and eats.

The interaction between Paul and Lisa quickly produced more entropy in their relationship. This kind of interaction had been common in their relationship before they learned about the downward spiral and how to change it. Paul and Lisa have changed a lot, but they are not perfect. There will always be some entropy in every marriage.

People come into my office expecting that I will be able to solve all their problems and that they will have a perfect relationship, but that's not going to happen. Nor do I believe there's a quick fix. Entropy always exists in varying degrees, depending on how much energy couples want to put into their relationships. Your job is to constantly identify it and battle it, as a team and as individuals.

Paul's and Lisa's Disputation

Compare this version of Paul's and Lisa's interaction with the first one. In this example, each tries to dispute his or her self talk. They try to identify their negative thoughts, and they test them against reality. They replace the distorted thoughts with more balanced, healthier thoughts, and the interaction changes.

Paul might tell himself, "Lisa's work at home is just as hard as mine. It is hard work being with children all day! Her remodeling projects are necessary because they make our house a home. Her projects are relatively inexpensive. Part of the cost will be realized in the sale of our home. It also makes Lisa happy. I'm imposing onto her my Spartan attitudes about buying things. I learned these things from my family, and it isn't fair to expect her to feel the same. I'm demanding that she be like me. Of course, this is irrational, because she could try to do the same to me, and I wouldn't like it. It's a wash. I need to give her some slack and not make a mountain out of a molehill."

Lisa might say, "Paul does love me. Saying he doesn't is an exaggeration. He may not understand parts of me. Maybe he's overreacting because he's had a bad day at work. We need to talk this out. He probably wouldn't do well all day with the children. I don't have to prove anything to Paul. I know who I am and what I'm about. I can't make him see me in a certain way."

Again, identifying and disputing your negative, irrational thoughts will help immensely in your marriage. It takes effort, and it can be frustrating to do. Check out the things that you're thinking with your spouse, to eliminate assumptions and misperceptions.

The Lockhorns, King Features Syndicate, Hoerst & Reiner. Used by permission. The writers of this strip have great insight into marital dynamics.

Chapter 5

Who Am I? My Identity in Christ

Christ emptied himself. Behold our pattern!
- St. Ambrose

Nothing is so strong as gentleness, nothing so gentle as strength.
- St. Francis de Sales

Then you will know the truth, and the truth will set you free.
- John 8:32 (NIVI)

In the last two chapters we have discussed the importance of what you tell yourself. Our self talk will have direct consequences in terms of our emotions, feelings, behaviors, and physical reactions. The connection between how we think and who we are is a critical link for each of us. "I think, therefore I am," wrote the philosopher René Descartes, and Proverbs 23:7 reminds us, "As a man thinks, so he is."

We have explored the dramatic effect of our upbringing in terms of the unrecognized assumptions we have transferred into our marriages, our parenting styles, and how we see the world. Negative or destructive messages will catalyze entropy in every marriage.

As individuals begin to analyze their self talk, they may start to see the irrational and distorted themes that clutter their minds. They often ask me, "How do I know if my self talk is distorted, and what do I do to change it?" These are cornerstone questions. As we have already seen, our thoughts and beliefs produce our emotions and feelings, which strongly influence our behaviors. So what are the answers to these critical questions?

How do we know if we are thinking negative thoughts, and what do we do to change them? As a Christian-based psychotherapist I would look to biblical truths for these answers. I would not recite to you a Bible verse for every problem. I think that approach can be spiritually abusive and damaging because you may think that you are not measuring up to a given Bible verse, principle, or spirituality. You might begin to feel that you have failed God, and consequently you pull away from God even more. Hence your problem may become worse. I don't believe that God works this way. In a way, the Bible-verse approach almost parallels the Old Testament use of the law. That is, people could begin to think that God's love and acceptance of them rests on their performance or how they measure up to a set of Bible verses.

I ask you to examine who you are as a person. Look at your beliefs about yourself, God, marriage, and family. Then begin to apply biblical truths with the assistance of the Holy Spirit.

Patty's Story

Although Patty had grown up in a strongly religious family, she had been extensively sexually abused as a young girl. She came to me for treatment of her depression. She also grew up believing it was her fault that she had been abused by a family member. Her parents had punished her for what they thought was Patty's part in the abuse when it was discovered. In other words, her authority figures punished her for being victimized.

Patty came to me when she was in her forties. She was married, with children, and she loved the Lord with all her heart. Yet she had entered adulthood with several distorted thoughts based on her family of origin beliefs. They included:

I dare not be honest, or I could be punished.

God can punish us even if we haven't been bad.

God will certainly punish us if we have been bad.

I need to keep up my guard with people; I can't let them in, or they will hurt me.

These distorted thoughts became entropy increasers in her marriage, because they had an impact on how she interacted with her husband. She was emotionally guarded with him, because being honest about her feelings and thoughts was almost impossible for her. She had to be prodded to talk about her thoughts. For many years she had based her life on these beliefs.

Patty lived in a state of uncertainty about herself and about other people and how they might treat her. She almost expected people not to like her; it was almost acceptable for people to mistreat her.

During one of our early sessions, Patty drew a sense of her picture of God. The picture showed a large lightning bolt coming out of the sky and striking a baby bird in a nest high in a tree. I interpreted this to mean that her perception was that she could never feel loved by God just for being Patty. Even in the warm, secure nest God could zap her at any time without notice. As a therapist I was able to understand the dynamics of why she saw God this way. Possibly it went back to when she was only six and her parents chastised her for being sexually abused. The abuse and punishment caused the little girl great emotional trauma. Yet, more than twenty-five years of sermons and Christian influence had not changed how she saw God. Why? The answer is that it is complicated to sort out a person's issues, identify his or her entropy increasers in marriage, and develop a healthy concept of God all at once.

Reciting a few Bible verses to her would have damaged Patty even more. Patty would tell herself that she was a failure, because she couldn't measure up to the verses. She might think a real Christian should let go of the past and move forward. Patty lived with her pain for many years. Chained by her cognitive distortions about herself, other people, and God, Patty lived a type of prison sentence within her mind. However, Patty's cognitive distortions made sense based on what she had experienced.

Recognizing Cognitive Distortions

Patty's therapy consisted initially of undoing her cognitive distortions. We were attempting to break the chain of cognitive distortion that held her back from being who she truly was. Patty was tired of living this prison sentence and wanted to break free.

Slowly Patty began to learn that her early sexual abuse had created her overly strong emotional guards, which in turn caused her to insulate herself from her husband and family. The emotional barrier that she had erected as a child was a defense mechanism to ensure her survival as a person. She learned that the parental punishment she had received for the sexual abuse was a type of revictimization, a form of postsexual abuse. She now understands that her parents thought what they were doing was right but that they made a tragic mistake in disciplining her. The state of constant uncertainty she felt, as a child and as an adult, was a result of this punishment. Being punished for a traumatic event that wasn't her fault instilled a lifelong sense of uncertainty. The constant assurances of her husband's love were not enough to break down this barrier. This state of mind had served as an entropy increaser. Patty had incorrectly learned that it was better to keep things to herself so she would not be attacked, judged, condemned, or criticized for expressing herself. With therapy, she began to understand how this had become an entropy increaser in her marriage.

Patty began to believe that God would not punish her randomly, without notice or warning, like a lightning bolt from the sky. She learned that this deep fear was also caused by the sexual abuse. Over the years she had asked herself many questions that had gone unanswered. She wondered why God would allow sexual abuse. Where was God during the abuse? Why weren't her parents protecting her? Why should anybody do something as terrible as sexual abuse? Why should she be punished when she told her parents the truth? Weren't they supposed to protect her from bad things? Maybe she was bad. Since she was bad, then God was punishing her. God was angry with her and didn't protect her from the abuse.

Her parents, in a sense, represented God to Patty. Their angry, punishing, judgmental attitude shaped Patty's negative view of God as distant, punishing, and judgmental. Since his punishment could strike randomly, without notice, Patty lived in state of constant tension and anxiety, which made her tired and chronically depressed. She tried to get God's approval but never knew how to do that. Because she had been made to feel that she was to blame for the abuse, she was deeply shame-based. She tried to look good on the outside, partly to avoid giving anyone ammunition to condemn her and partly to look good to God. Patty began to realize that this approach was empty; it gave her nothing while tiring her out. But her cognitive distortions were so great that she did not know what was true and what was distorted. Patty was slowly dying on the inside, and nobody knew it.

As we worked together, Patty began to learn that God loves her for who she is. God knows we are defective, weak, and sinful, but God loves us anyway. She learned that she didn't have to put up a wall with other people or with God, and she could be more transparent. She saw that sometimes relationships can be painful and that sometimes those who love us can hurt us the most, either intentionally or unintentionally. Bad things can happen, but so can good things. She began to believe that God would not send a lightning bolt to strike her. She began to believe that God wants to hold her, secure and warm, in his gracious love. Patty learned she does not have to measure up to certain standards of conduct, behavior, or other perceptions of performance in order to gain God's love. Patty was beginning to understand and accept grace. This allowed Patty to rest, relax, and drop her guard. This was a process that took time as Patty sorted out her issues.

Patty also came to believe that she wasn't a bad or disgusting person, as she had previously thought. Her religious teaching had always told her that she was made in God's image, and now she began to believe that teaching. Because of that, she learned and believed she was special and valuable and that she had gifts, talents, and abilities. Patty is a warm, wonderful person with much to offer her family and others around her.

This kind of self-discovery takes time. Western culture tends to be result-oriented, and because of this we come to expect our needs and desires to be met quickly. We can become impatient with ourselves or with others if change does not occur rapidly enough for us. For example, we Christians put a lot of emphasis on salvation (which we should), yet at times we put little emphasis on our spiritual journey with God after the conversion experience. Just as our walk with God never ends, so entropy is an issue that will not go away.

Our Christianity, regardless of denomination, becomes the ultimate source of our values. These values in turn become an integral part of our thoughts. These Christian, value-driven thoughts produce our emotions and influence our behaviors. The idea of Christianity driving our thoughts or serving as our underlying philosophy or ideology is a lifetime process of realization.

Who we are in Christ, along with our Christian principles, is at our center, and from that they influence us in all spheres of our lives. Our thoughts determine our behaviors and our emotions. This is the key to everything; it is a supporting pillar in our lives. Our thoughts determine how we view our jobs, how we treat coworkers, how we deal with friends, how we vote, how we stand on various issues, our participation in our communities, how we spend our money, and on the kinds of churches we attend and our level of involvement. It affects how we view our children and thus our parenting styles, how we see our relatives and our extended families, and how we see our marriages. Who we are in Christ determines how we operate in our marriage. Our relationship with Jesus permeates our essence and how we think and operate (see fig. 8).

Figure 8

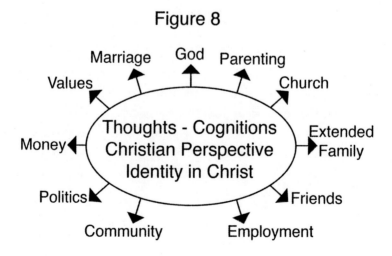

I believe that a Christian perspective will help to define your thoughts in various areas of your life, including marriage. Chapter 6 will delineate a perspective in marriage that can help you decrease entropy. It is essential to know more about who you are in Jesus Christ, as this will help restructure any distorted thoughts that you may have about yourself. This is an ongoing, lifetime process between you and God. I would encourage you to find a church that is comfortable for you, if you don't already attend one. Find one that feeds you with God's word, teaches God's love and acceptance of you, and challenges you in your walk with God.

Questions for You and Your Spouse to Answer and Discuss

1. Who are you in Christ?
2. What are your Christian values, and how do they influence your behaviors and emotions?
3. Are you grace-oriented or performance-oriented, and why?
4. How has your upbringing influenced how you see God?
5. How do you incorporate your spirituality and understanding of God in your marriage?

Bible Verses Related to Our Identity in Christ[1]
Genesis 1:31
Genesis 5:1-2
1 Samuel 16:7
Psalm 8:4-6

---

[1]. "Who We Are," *Minirth Meier Clinic Magazine* (fall 1989): 3. Most of the verses were from this article. The selection of verses only scratches the surface as to your identity in Christ.

Psalm 18:28-29
Psalm 27:10
Psalm 37:3-7, 23-24
Psalm 139
Proverbs 3:5-6
Romans 11:18
Proverbs 15:15
Proverbs 23:7
Isaiah 61:10
Matthew 6:25-33
Matthew 7:11
Matthew 10:29-31
John 15:1-5
John 17:23
Romans 4:8
Romans 5:8, 11
Romans 8
Romans 12:1-8
1 Corinthians 10:13
2 Corinthians 5:20
2 Corinthians 12:9-10
Ephesians 1:3-6
Ephesians 2:5-19, 18-22
Philippians 2:1-4, 13
Philippians 4:11-13
Hebrews 13:5-6
1 Peter 1:15-16
1 Peter 4:10-11
1 John 4:7-21

I encourage you to look up these verses and ask yourself how they apply to you. Try to understand how God sees you from this perspective. Remember to use these passages as your pattern of correct information when you cognitively restructure your thoughts from distortions about God. Doing our best to live in the truth helps to free us from past issues and perceptions. It reinforces what Jesus said in John 8:32 (NIVI): "Then you will know the truth, and the truth will set you free."

Chapter 6

Husband and Wife: Partnership, Service, Regency

The ideal state of marriage is a reflection of the symbiotic nature and relationship of the Trinity.

- Brian Nystrom

Many of my male clients have told me, "She's my wife—the Bible says a wife should submit to her husband and give him sex when he wants it." Or they say, "She should do things the way I tell her, because the Bible says I'm in charge." Some women wonder whether they must submit to their husbands in these and other matters. Often a man will claim that Ephesians 5:22 ("Wives, submit to your husbands as to the Lord," NIVI) teaches that he has a right to rule over his wife. He often assumes it means he has sole rule over the family, too. People base many teachings on the husbands' supposed headship, and some of them will cite Genesis 3:16 as teaching a leading role for the husband: "And he will rule over you" (NIVI).

How these verses are interpreted is vital, because we have seen that whatever we tell ourselves will determine our behaviors, emotions, and feelings. Therefore, our perspective on roles in marriage will determine how we interact with and treat our spouses. Our perspective on marriage roles stems from several factors, including our family experiences, cultural influences, personal experiences in relationships, and our understanding of theology and Scripture. I have found there are three general perspectives, or models, of marriage. As we explore each model, ask yourself where your own marriage fits into this framework.

Garden of Eden Model of Marriage

To understand this model of marriage, we must first look to Genesis. In Genesis 1:26–28 (NIVI) we read:

> Then God said, "Let us make human beings in our image, according to our likeness, and let them rule over the fish of the sea and over the birds of the air, over the livestock, over all the earth, and over all the creatures that move along the ground."
>
> So God created human beings
>   in his own image,
> in the image of God
>   he created them;
> male and female
>   he created them.
>
> God blessed them and said to them, "Be fruitful and increase in number; fill the earth and subdue it. Rule over the fish of the sea and the birds of the air and over every living thing that moves on the ground."

Further, in Genesis 2:18, 20–25 (NIVI), we read:

> The LORD God said, "It is not good for the man to be alone. I will make a helper suitable for him."…So the man gave names to all the livestock, the birds of the air and the beasts of the field.

But for Adam no suitable helper was found. So the LORD God caused the man to fall into a deep sleep; and while he was sleeping, he took one of the man's ribs and closed up the place with flesh. Then the LORD God made a woman from the rib he had taken out of the man, and he brought her to the man. The man said,

"This is now bone of my bones
    and flesh of my flesh;
she shall be called 'woman,'
    for she was taken out of man."

For this reason a man will leave his father and mother and be united to his wife, and they will become one flesh.

The man and his wife were both naked, and they felt no shame.

These passages tell me that before the fall and the curse, God's original design for marriage was one of man and woman ruling together, side by side in partnership. Genesis 1:26 talks about Adam and Eve ruling over everything. Nowhere in these passages does the Bible say that Adam ruled over Eve or vice versa.

In the Hebrew, Genesis 1:26 reads, "Let us make *ha'adam* in our image," and *ha'adam* means "human being," not just "man."[1] There are profound ramifications if we read verse 26 in this way. To say anything less reduces the

---

[1.] Based on personal discussions with Dr. Joy Elasky Fleming. See her *Man and Woman in Biblical Unity—Theology form Genesis 2–3*. This book, abstracted from her doctoral dissertation, examines the Hebrew of Genesis 2–3 and supports biblical equality between men and women. Her doctoral dissertation, *A Rhetorical Analysis of Genesis 2–3 with Implications for a Theology of Man and Woman* (Strasbourg: University of Strasbourg,1987), provides scholarly detail.

value of females and is not what God intended or created. Ultimately, an interpretation that excludes women will affect one's marriage.

Genesis 1:27 tells us that Adam and Eve were both created in the image of God. This is a crucial verse for us as we try to understand our incredible personal worth—we are all, male and female, made in God's image. Genesis 2:22–23 says that the woman was formed from man, but Scripture does not give Adam more authority because of this.

The Hebrew words used in Genesis 2:18 and 20 are *'ezer kenegdo*. A literal translation of this phrase is "A help corresponding to him."[2] The word *'ezer* could connote someone coming to the rescue, one who has superior strength. Instead of Eve being thought of as weaker because she was made from Adam, it could be argued that she had strength that Adam needed. The word *kenegdo* means "like him, and in front of or facing him." Therefore Eve was formed from Adam and had at least equal strength and essence. They are face to face. In order to be face to face, two people must be at the same level. This phrasing means that there was no difference in rank between Adam and Eve. It also speaks of closeness and intimacy between them. I believe it is fair to say that God's original design was that Adam and Eve were equal partners, with the same essence; neither had power over the other, and there was a harmonious closeness between them.

In Genesis 2:24–25 we see that a man is to leave his parents and create a new family with his wife when he marries. The Scriptures use the Hebrew word *dabaq*, meaning "cleaves, clings, or keeps close," to describe the husband's relationship with his wife. The strength of the verb *dabaq* expresses great personal loyalty, commitment, and emotional closeness, as well as the exclusivity of the marriage covenant between one man and one woman.[3]

---

2. Ibid.
3. Ibid.

What had been one, Adam, became two, Adam and Eve. In marriage the two become one (Genesis 2:24) through a partnership based on their becoming "one flesh." They were *'ezer kenegdo,* of equal essence and strength in a face-to-face, equal position, and they had become joined in a one-flesh marriage. The best word I can think of to describe this relationship is a partnership. Both husband and wife are equal and rule together, but they are subservient to God (see fig. 9).

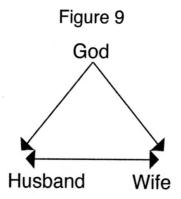

Figure 9

In this partnership model, I would imagine that Adam and Eve made decisions together and consulted with each other on everything. They would have communicated well, and one would not have ordered the other around. They did not selfishly meet their own needs at the expense of the other. They encouraged each other, and they spent time together. I visualize a marriage bond that was so close and mutually caring that they were inseparable—like one flesh. In a bond like this, it doesn't matter who's "in charge" because each party is so focused on the other that the needs and wants of both are naturally respected. Each partner respects the unique individuality of the other person.

I think this is what God had in mind when he created Adam and Eve. In a sense, a tight, intimate partnership like this resembles some of the complex dynamics of the Trinity. Genesis 1:26a alludes to this when it says "in our likeness." The Trinity displays co-equality among the three persons, and although there are distinct persons in the Trinity, they are one. The husband-wife partnership displays co-equality between two persons, and though there are two distinct persons in the partnership, they are one. There is a parallel between a Christian-based marriage and the Trinity. In a Christian marriage, both partners are one, both rule together, yet each person is distinct (see fig. 10)

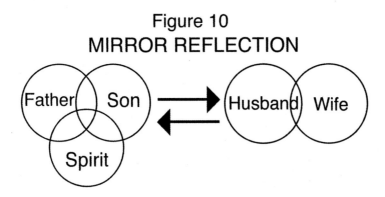

Figure 10
MIRROR REFLECTION

The Garden of Eden model of marriage is a model to look to for our own marriages, but everything in this perfect marriage changed (Genesis 3).

The Sin Era of Marriage

In the next model of marriage, we look at what changed after the fall. We all know the story of Genesis 3—of how the serpent deceived Eve into eating the fruit that God had commanded them not to eat. Eve then offered it to Adam, and he also ate it. As a result of this disobedience (Genesis 3:14–19 NIVI),

> So the LORD God said to the serpent, "Because you have done this,
>
> "Cursed are you above all the livestock
>   and all the wild animals!
> You will crawl on your belly
>   and you will eat dust
>   all the days of your life.
> And I will put enmity
>   between you and the woman,
>   and between your offspring and hers;
> he will crush your head,
>   and you will strike his heel."
>
> To the woman he said,
>
> "I will greatly increase your pains in childbearing;
>   with pain you will give birth to children.
> Your desire will be for your husband,
>   and he will rule over you."
>
> To Adam he said, "Because you listened to your wife and ate from the tree about which I commanded you, 'You shall not eat of it,'
>
> "Cursed is the ground because of you;
>   through painful toil shall you eat of it
>   all the days of your life.
> It will produce thorns and thistles for you,
>   and you will eat the plants of the field.
> By the sweat of your brow
>   you will eat your food
> until you return to the ground,
>   since from it you were taken;
> for dust you are,
>   and to dust you will return."

This story describes the fall from the perfect state to being corrupted by sin. This set the course for our minds and bodies to deteriorate and to be corrupted. This is the cause of aberrant, negative, or distorted cognitive perceptions. This is the beginning of physical and mental illness, as well as spiritual death. In Genesis 3:11–12 (NIVI), we see the beginnings of marital discord, when God asked Adam if he had eaten from the tree. Instead of giving God a direct answer, Adam replied, "The woman you put here with me—she gave me some fruit from the tree, and I ate it." In an aggressive way, Adam blamed God and Eve and did not take responsibility for his own action. He had a difficult time admitting fault. He blamed God for giving him Eve. He blamed Eve for giving him the fruit. Adam was arrogant and disobedient to God by going against God's directive and also by blaming God for giving him Eve, who had been his equal, one-flesh partner.

In Genesis 3:13 we see how Eve was more candid with God. She accurately identified the serpent for deceiving her but then admitted that she ate the fruit. Genesis 3:1–5 shows us how the serpent, who had been animated by Satan, deceived her. Eve did not blame God for her actions, as her husband did. She correctly identified the serpent, who was the mouthpiece of Satan, as the one who maliciously deceived her into eating the fruit. Both Adam and Eve knew of God's directive not to eat from the tree (Genesis 2:16–17; 3:2-3) or they would die. It is easy to understand that due to the closeness of the one-flesh partnership, each partner influenced the other, with the result that both sinned. Adam could have said no, and Eve could have done the same.

This story illustrates the first example of marital blame and failure to take responsibility for one's actions. Many times in marital relationships, people have difficulty admitting fault or taking responsibility for things, as the comic strip "The Lockhorns" portrays (see cartoon 2). This was dysfunctional for Adam, and it is still dysfunctional. In a healthy marriage, in which people are actively working on reducing entropy, it is important to acknowledge when we're wrong and to apologize to our partners for our mistakes.

THE LOCKHORNS

"I'M JUST HERE TO FIND OUT WHAT LORETTA'S PROBLEM IS."

I have often wondered if gender-related tendencies go back to Adam and Eve. That is, are men more defensive, more guarded, and more blaming? Are men less in touch with their feelings and women more in touch with them? Are women more honest and open, more accurate in their descriptions of interpersonal relationships? Any answer would be speculative and open to debate, but I see these dynamics played out in marriages time after time. This is not to say that women are never defensive, guarded, or blaming. Both genders share these challenges. I am saying that women generally have shown more skill at interpersonal relationships than have men. Women tend to be more focused on relationship issues than are men. Men, like Adam, have been more detached, where women are more relational. These are of course generalizations. Many men have put energy into transforming their marriages, self-awareness, and interpersonal skills.

Adam and Eve's equal partnership best illustrates God's original design for marriage. Some of you reading this may be asking, "What about the man being in charge? That's God's design." I believe there is no scriptural evidence that prior to the fall Adam was to rule over Eve. Genesis 1 and 2 state that Adam and Eve were to rule "together, jointly."

Another strong argument supporting a partnership model is Genesis 3:16, which states that one of the consequences of sin is that "he will rule" over the woman. If God had intended Adam to rule over Eve in the Garden of Eden, why didn't he say so in Genesis 1 and 2? Genesis 3:16 implies that some other condition was in place prior to the fall. Otherwise Genesis 3:16 would not describe Adam ruling over Eve as a consequence of sinful behavior. If Adam and Eve had not committed the original sin, then their existence would not have changed, and the principles in place prior to the fall would have continued. That is, their perfect marriage and their perfect existence would have continued indefinitely. God's ideal was and is always there. Or sin distorts God's ideal of marriage.

In *Man and Woman in Biblical Unity—Theology from Genesis 2–3,* Dr. Joy Elasky Fleming writes that Eve missed her previous equal partnership that she enjoyed with Adam before the fall.[4] She missed the intense one-flesh relationship that they once shared. Adam's ruling over Eve was not a prescription from God but a description of what would happen in the male-female relationship as a result of sin. Adam took advantage of the situation and established himself over Eve in a hierarchical fashion. Adam chose to distance himself from God's sovereignty over him.

As we look at the beginning of marital blame in Genesis 3:12, when Adam blames Eve and God for his own disobedience, we see the ugly effects of sin.

---

4. Ibid.

These include the shame-and-blame combination resulting from disobeying God's directive and the ensuing difficulty in accepting ownership of sin. These are the beginnings of marital entropy that did not exist before the fall. Adam and Eve had gone from a close, equal partnership to a distant, entropy-laden marriage marked by Adam blaming Eve and Eve sorely missing the close partnership that had previously existed (see fig. 11).

Figure 11

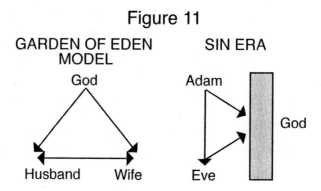

We can still see the societal consequences of this hierarchical thinking. In many cultures women are considered the property of their husbands. There is still more celebration of the birth of a boy than of a girl. Some wives still feel bad if they don't give their husbands sons (even though the male chromosome determines the gender of the baby). In many families the parents will encourage and pay for a son's college education but will not do the same for a daughter. Daughters are still sometimes told they should count on getting married to support themselves, and schools and parents still point young women toward nurturing or support roles rather than technical or leadership positions.

The fall has negative ramifications for all societies. Even if we look only at the consequences of sin, of man ruling over woman, this attitude of male superiority has allowed men to feel justified or excused in committing crimes against women. These include domestic violence (physical, sexual, or emotional violence), rape, and assault. When men think that they are better than women we also see evidence of this attitude in the marketplace. Women are still paid considerably less than men are for equivalent work; men control most corporations, including boards of directors. Even today, young girls are mutilated in female circumcision, without benefit of anesthesia or sanitary conditions, in many parts of Africa, the Middle East, Southeast Asia, and South America. This practice is believed to date back more than four thousand years and holds that an intact woman is dirty, oversexed, and unmarriageable.

I have seen many men who regard themselves as better, smarter, and superior to their wives. I have seen husbands constantly invalidate their wives, catalyzing entropy. I have seen many wives deeply hurt by the actions of their husbands. I have seen many wives accept abuse from their husbands because they thought their role was to "take it and be submissive." I don't think God intended wives to be doormats. God created and intended women to be equal to men in all aspects of life, as we have seen in the Garden of Eden model of marriage.

Redemption Era of Marriage

In Romans 6:6–9 (NIVI) we find a third model of marriage:

> For we know that our old self was crucified with him so that the body of sin might be done away with, that we should no longer be slaves to sin—for anyone who has died has been freed from sin.

> Now if we died with Christ, we believe that we will also live with him. For we know that since Christ was raised from the dead, he cannot die again; death no longer has mastery over him.

Romans 6 tells us that our old selves are crucified with Christ and that our old, sinful ways might be left behind us. We live by the Holy Spirit, who is writing God's love and ways into our hearts. We are guided in our daily lives by the Holy Spirit who lives within us, by God's Word, and by our identities in Christ. What does this mean in the context of a marriage?

We can rejoice that Christ redeemed us. Faith in Christ causes the Holy Spirit to dwell in each believer. Let's look at the New Testament to begin to understand the redemption era of marriage, in particular the passage in Ephesians 5.

This chapter has been widely quoted as validating the hierarchy found in the sin era model of marriage. Many people have used Ephesians 5:22–24 to teach that wives must be subordinate to their husbands in all things, at all times, without question. This sounds like the sin model of marriage, but Jesus removed us from the bondage of sin. He gives us the freedom to reexamine how our relationships will work; he shows us the path back toward God's original design.

Perhaps a careful analysis of Ephesians 5:15–33 (NIVI) will help us to understand how to apply this passage to modern marriages. It is important to look at the entire passage to understand what the apostle Paul meant when he wrote it. It is also important to remember that in these verses, Paul uses an analogy of how husbands and wives relate to each other to illustrate how members of the church are to relate to one another.

> Be very careful, then, how you live—not as unwise but as wise, making the most of every opportunity, because the days are evil. Therefore do not be foolish, but understand what the Lord's will is. Do not get drunk on wine, which leads to debauchery. Instead, be filled with the Spirit. Speak to one another with psalms, hymns and spiritual songs. Sing and make music in your heart to the Lord,

always giving thanks to God the Father for everything, in the name of our Lord Jesus Christ.

Submit to one another out of reverence for Christ.

Wives, submit to your husbands as to the Lord. For the husband is the head of the wife as Christ is the head of the church, his body, of which he is the Savior. Now as the church submits to Christ, so also wives should submit to their husbands in everything.

Husbands, love your wives, just as Christ loved the church and gave himself up for her to make her holy, cleansing her by the washing of water through the word, and to present her to himself as a radiant church, without stain or wrinkle or any other blemish, but holy and blameless. In this same way, husbands ought to love their wives as their own bodies. He who loves his wife loves himself. After all, people have never hated their own bodies, but feed and care for them, just as Christ does the church—for we are members of the body. "For this reason a man will leave his father and mother and be united to his wife, and the two will become one flesh." This is a profound mystery—but I am talking about Christ and the church. However, each one of you also must love his wife as he loves himself, and the wife must respect her husband.

I believe this passage tells use several important things.[5] It describes a Christian church, full of praise for the Lord. Paul describes how careful Christians are to walk. He tells them how they should treat each other in their making, speaking, giving, and submitting to each other. In verse 21, Paul tells us that the husband and wife are subject to one another in the

---

5. Personal discussions with Dr. Bruce Fleming about the Greek and corresponding English translation of Ephesians 5 helped to clarify the section on the redemption era model of marriage.

fear of Christ. This is a major change from the sin era model of marriage, in which sinful husbands ruled over their wives as an outgrowth of sin. Christ has removed that sin, and a husband and wife can subject themselves graciously to one another, with both being subject to God.

As we see so often in Scripture, God's Word often includes one or several analogies to make it easier for us to understand. Although verses 22 through 24 may have been misused to support the roles of a dominant husband and a subordinate wife, they are an extension of verse 21, which commands that the husband and wife be subject to one another. Since Paul's words in verse 21 demonstrate equality between spouses, he is able to use interchangeable words.

A glance at the Greek words behind the English shows that Paul modifies the hierarchical concept of submitting to someone in charge. Verse 21 says "submitting to one another," and in verse 22 there is no verb, which means that the reader is to apply the verb from verse 21. The picture is of husbands and wives mutually submitting, and this serves as an illustration of how believers—all believers—are to treat each other. Paul confirms this understanding in verse 32, where he reminds readers that he has been talking about Christ and the church. What a beautiful picture of life in the body of Christ![6]

In verse 25 Paul shifts to a second analogy: the way Christ loves the church. This verse makes a daring departure from the near master-slave relationship that existed during the sin era. Paul commands husbands that they must love their wives. In fact, he tells them they must love their wives as much as Christ showed his love for the church when he sacrificed himself for its good. It was a radical notion that a husband should love his wife sacrificially, when previously he had only to rule her.

---

6. Ibid.

This theme continues in verses 26 and 27, in which Paul describes the degree to which Christ worked to sanctify the church. By analogy, he is saying that a husband is expected to work hard to treat his wife in such a way as to demonstrate how special and important she is. The husband must not treat her in a way that would blemish her, just as Christ would do nothing to harm the church in any way. A man's task is to direct his heart toward God, anchor his identity in Christ, and dispute his cognitive distortions—and he must learn to do these all at the same time he is interacting with his wife. This ongoing process will help her to feel loved and cared about. He might even see a brief reflection of how the Trinity operates and how much God loves us and accepts us for who we are.

The idea of treating other believers in the church in a mutually submissive way was so different from the world the Ephesians lived in that Paul elaborates in verses 28 through 30. To make sure that he is understood, Paul again tells husbands to love their wives. This time he says the husbands must love their wives as much as they love their own bodies. He reminds us that we are all members of the body of Christ.

Paul is phrasing his words in a way that the Ephesians will be able to understand. First, he tells them that a wife and husband are subject to one another in the fear of Christ, and he restates this so he is certain they will know what he means. Since wives were accustomed to being subject to their husbands, they needed only a brief reminder. But to the husbands, being subject to their wives was a foreign concept, and Paul needed to explain what "being subject" means. It means that a husband will love his wife so much that he would be willing to sacrifice himself for her. A love that strong would take into account the wife's wishes, and husbands would learn to treat their wives so well that they would be without blemish.

To make certain there is no misunderstanding Paul goes further in verse 31 to instruct the man that he must leave his father and mother when he marries and form a new family with his wife. His loyalty, devotion, and effort are put into his marriage.

Paul summarized in verse 33 by repeating himself. A man, he says, must love his wife as he does himself. If a man loves himself, does that mean he disrespects himself? Does it mean he would treat himself badly? Or does it mean that he would treat himself—and by extension, his wife—with respect? That's the point. Paul goes out of his way to tell husbands to love their wives, with all the various meanings of the word *love*. For women, more accustomed to paying respect to their husbands, he simply tells them to continue to do so.

Taken in context, Paul's message is clear: be subject to one another, with mutual submission before God. Love and respect each other. It sounds easy, doesn't it? But these passages traditionally have been interpreted to mean that a husband should continue to rule his wife. But if we look at these verses as a unit, we can see that it is time to reclaim God's original design for marriage. Our marriage models have come full circle (see fig. 12).

Figure 12

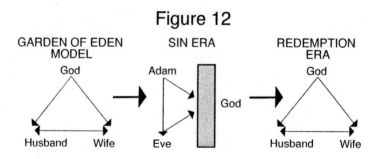

| GARDEN OF EDEN MODEL | SIN ERA | REDEMPTION ERA |

Partnership, Service, Regency

Now we can refer to the Garden of Eden and redemption models of marriage by a more descriptive term, the Partnership-Service-Regency (PSR) model. The beliefs that support this model drive and determine our behaviors and emotions as we interact in marriage.

Partnership refers to the equal footing a husband and wife have together before God and before each other. They are exclusive life partners facing and dealing with all of their problems and joys together. They leave their parents and become as one flesh. They have a common essence as humans.

Service refers to the mutual submission, love, sacrifice, nurturing, and cherishing qualities in marriage. In Ephesians Paul uses the church as an illustration of how marriages ought to be and points back to God's original design.

Regency refers to the directive of ruling together (Genesis 1 and 2) over all. The husband and wife rule over their dominion together. One does not rule over the other.

Questions for You and Your Spouse to Answer and Discuss

1. What model has described your marriage, and why?
2. What would need to change, or is left to change, to more fully integrate the PSR model into your marriage?
3. What would prevent this from happening?
4. Discuss what the Garden of Eden model would have been like for Adam and Eve before the fall.

Chapter 7

Pushing Your Spouse Away: Desanctification

"In your anger do not sin."
- Ephesians 4:26 (NIVI)

Violence in any form—physical, sexual, psychological or verbal—is sinful.
1. U.S. Catholic bishops

In chapter 6 we looked at the Partnership-Service-Regency (PSR) model of marriage, which has ramifications for every aspect of a marriage. If the husband are wife are co-equal, how does this determine the workings of their relationship day to day? How should each partner treat the other person? The opposite question is also important: How should each partner not treat the other person?

We can draw from many Bible passages to help us reshape our thinking patterns regarding our relationship. We will begin by looking again at Ephesians 5:25–27. Remember Ephesians 5 discusses the church and how members of the body of Christ are to treat one another. Paul uses the church as an illustration of how husbands and wives are to relate to each other:

Husbands, love your wives, just as Christ also loved the church and gave himself up for her; that he might sanctify her, having cleansed her by the washing of water with the word, that he might present to himself the church in all her glory, having no spot or wrinkle or any such thing; but that she should be holy and blameless.

In these verses I see a glimpse of how the Trinity operates and that marriage, ideally, can reflect this. To learn to reflect the Trinity in your own marriage, you must first come to understand the concept of marital sanctification.

Marital sanctification is the process of integrating the skills the we have already discussed: constantly balancing our self talk, being aware of how our upbringing influences our marriage, knowing who we are in Christ, and understanding the PSR model of marriage. Remember, your thoughts determine your feelings and emotions and influence you behavior. All of this is a process of understanding the concepts, thinking, praying to God for guidance, and acting out the beliefs with your spouse on a day-to-day basis.

We will return to the subject of sanctification in chapter 8, which includes a discussion of marriage needs, love, and commitment. Before we can understand sanctification, it will help if we look at the opposite concept: desanctification. This is because all of us at times desanctify our spouses, and we need to know what desanctification is, how to identify it, what to do with it, and how to reconcile with our spouses as a result of it.

In this context, desanctification means treating a spouse in any way that means he or she does not feel set apart or special. It includes attitudes, beliefs, actions, or behaviors that create a spot or wrinkle on our spouses or on our marriages. Desanctifying actions, behaviors, attitudes, or beliefs increase entropy and push spouses apart (see fig. 13).

Figure 13
ENTROPY

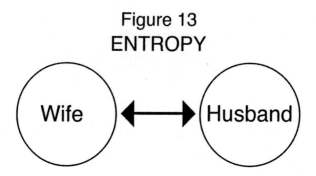

We can identify fourteen general categories of desanctifying behaviors, and remember that specific behaviors may cross into other categories (see fig. 14)). For example, some kinds of threats might be considered psychological abuse; swearing is both verbal abuse and profanity. It is impossible to list every specific desanctifying behavior for each category.

Figure 14
Desanctification Cycle

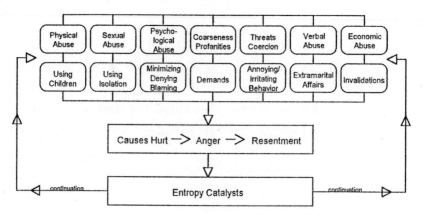

All desanctifying behaviors cause hurt, anger, and resentment. If you desanctify your spouse, it will cause these feelings and increase entropy. Your spouse will pull away from you, and that distancing may manifest itself physically, emotionally, or sexually. The goal is to identify desanctification as rapidly as possible and stop it. The sooner this is done, with an apology to your spouse, the more it will prevent or reduce the degree of hurt, anger, and resentment.

As you read about desanctifying behaviors, ask yourself if you see any evidence of them in your marriage. Have you ever behaved this way with your spouse? Does your spouse behave in this way? What was the situation? How often does the behavior happen? Have you tried, as an individual or a couple, to stop the behavior? What self talk produces the action? What would it take to stop this behavior?

Read the following material with your guard down and your heart open to change. If there are desanctifications that you can identify, use that as a starting point to make a change. Desanctifications obstruct the essence and beauty of the PSR model of marriage.

Desanctifying Behaviors

Psychological abuse is more subtle than physical or sexual abuse, but it can be no less damaging. Persistent manipulation of intentions, promises, threats, inducing guilt, or any method that allows one spouse to gain something at the expense of the other are all instances of psychological abuse. For example, a spouse may promise to do something or change a behavior but then not follow through, minimizing or denying that the promise was made or that it was "just a joke." Or, a spouse may try to shame or place guilt on the other spouse for not meeting one's needs exactly when and how one wants. Making an accusation that is difficult or impossible to prove is psychological abuse, as are constant threats, spoken or unspoken, of one spouse abandoning the other. Continued reminders that an affair with someone who is more fun, more attractive, more understanding, more [fill in the blank] are also psychological abuse.

Spiritual abuse happens when one spouse mistreats the other through coercion, control, manipulation, or exploitation, with the result being spiritual wounds. This behavior is intended to show the spiritual superiority of one spouse over the other. Examples include using spirituality to control or dominate the other person; making disparaging comments about the other person's spirituality (e.g., "a real Christian leader would…"); attacking or belittling the other spouse's belief or doctrines; degrading or shaming the other spouse for not having one's own convictions about certain standards or conduct; or quoting Bible verses to gain at the other's expense.

Threats or coercion create fear and pressure to do something that one doesn't want to do. Verbal threats, driving at high speed or recklessly (against your spouse's wishes), or persistent verbal pressure to have sex are examples.

Verbal abuse is words that are intended to hurt, malign, or put down the other spouse. This includes unwanted foul language, such as swearing, cursing, offensive slang, sexually laden jokes, or other verbalisms that a spouse finds undesirable. Examples are yelling; lecturing—essentially saying "I know more than you do, and I'm going to make sure you know it"; verbal barrages, such as "I'm stuck with you; no one else would ever want you"; disparaging the other's abilities (intellect or skills) or characteristics (physical attributes or personality traits).

Economic abuse involves one spouse controlling the money, assets, or financial information in the marriage and excluding the other spouse.

Criticisms of the other spouse's expenditures when it is agreed that spouse is responsible for this area (e.g., groceries, children's clothes, car maintenance) is one example. Other examples are enforcing a double standard in which the critical spouse is not held accountable for his or her purchases while the other spouse is; withholding financial information, including such things as income, expenditures, savings, or investments; demanding that one's spouse should yield his or her paychecks, gifts, checkbook, or credit cards; or failing to involve one's spouse in financial decisions regarding savings plans, investments, or important purchases.

Using children may mean using them as tools against one's spouse or being abusive to the children directly. These tactics include holding unrealistic expectations, persistent or unwanted behaviors toward the children, behaviors that have not been agreed upon, or demands that involve the children. The essential point is that one parent persistently does or does not parent as the couple agreed to parent. Specific examples might include types of punishment with which one's spouse does not agree, excessive yelling at the children or calling them names, withholding privileges or items without the agreement of one's spouse, absence or minimal parenting involvement of one spouse, or physical abuse of the children or use of physical force on them.

Using isolation is a subtle maneuver, perhaps so subtle that the spouse may not realize what is happening. It includes persistent words or behaviors designed to prevent one spouse from developing or maintaining a network of friends or extended family. It makes the isolated spouse dependent on the other spouse, because that spouse has cut off contact with anyone who could advise or help.

Minimizing, denying, blaming or demanding is one spouse's inability or unwillingness to look at his or her contribution to problems, and this dynamic frequently exists in shame-based individuals (see chapter

2). By making a demand, the person is implying that she or he has the power to enforce the demand. This may be in either one's self talk or in an overt demand.

An example of a demand made in one's self talk would be a husband who tells himself that he must have sexual relations with his wife on a given night. When she declines, he becomes angry. His anger might be expressed in various ways: they might argue, he might sulk, or he might leave the bedroom.

An overt demand would be if one spouse persisted in a behavior toward the other, in which one was gaining and the other was not, or it might be an explicit demand to "do this or that."

Annoying, irritating or offending one's spouse describes subtle and often maddening things that spouses can do to annoy one another. Or they may be persistent behaviors or addictions that a spouse finds bothersome or offensive. Examples would be poor hygiene (bad breath, refusing to brush one's teeth, wearing dirty clothing, bathing infrequently); flirting with the opposite sex; mental illness for which the spouse refuses treatment; or addictions such as chemical dependency, gambling, smoking, or use of pornography, for which the spouse refuses treatment.

Addictions can be treated. If you are experiencing this desanctification, your spouse should have an evaluation completed by a licensed professional. These serious problems require professional help, because they debilitate the person, the marriage, and the family.

Having an *affair*, defined as having a romantic or sexual relationship with someone other than your spouse, is a commonly recognized signal that something is very wrong in a marriage. This is a seriously desanctifying behavior from which a marriage may never fully recover. Survivors of affairs tell me that it is difficult to redevelop the same level of trust within the marriage.

Invalidations can be defined as any words, behaviors, or actions that deny a spouse's perception of reality at a given moment. Invalidations can occur by denying a point the other spouse is trying to make; minimizing something that the other spouse is sharing; not giving the other spouse time or energy to discuss a given issue; ignoring the other spouse's opinion on certain issues; avoiding talking about an issue; telling a spouse he or she is wrong without first talking about the issue; putting down a spouse in front of others; lecturing, ridiculing, or making fun of a spouse; or dominating the conversation so that the other spouse is not given the opportunity or encouragement to share his or her thoughts.

Physical abuse is any action or threat of physically touching or hurting your spouse. The tendency toward physical abuse is found in all age groups and cuts across all racial, ethnic, economic, religious, occupational, and educational boundaries. More than a quarter of married people report physical abuse occurring in their marriages, but sociologist Murray Strauss stated that the "true incidence rate is probably closer to 50 or 60% of all couples than it is to 28% who are willing to describe the violent acts."[1]

Denial, shame, embarrassment, and fear of legal prosecution keep abusers and their victims from being honest about it. An abuse victim will often minimize the abuse and will not consider it bad enough to call the police. She might fear that her husband will seek revenge on her if she presses charges or if she physically separates from him.

---

1. Richard J. Gelles and Suzanne K. Steinmetz, *Behind Closed Doors; Violence in the American Family* (New York: Anchor Press/Doubleday, 1980). This was a comprehensive family violence research project measuring levels and degrees of violence in the home, and its social causes.

One instance of any of these behaviors constitutes physical abuse: threatening physical abuse ("I'll give you something to really cry about"); hitting, slapping, pushing, or kicking; pulling hair; restraining any body part; spitting on a spouse; threatening by pulling a punch; wrestling that's not playful; throwing objects in anger; attacking anyone with objects; physical manifestations of a temper tantrum, such as jumping up and down, door slamming, or punching a wall; or threatening to use weapons.

Research supports the idea that physical violence is a cyclical reaction and is not random; seldom does someone commit a serious act of violence without showing some indications beforehand. There is an atmosphere of desanctification in the marriage that shows a build-up toward an actual abusive behavior.[2] For a spouse to be abusive even once shows that his or her self talk is geared in such a way as to have produced the abusive behavior. When our self talk is producing physical abuse, we will see other desanctifying behaviors before the physical abuse happens.

No one ever deserves to be the victim of physical or sexual abuse. This is a criminal offense. If there is a pattern of abuse and the abuser denies the problem or refuses help, I would recommend a physical separation until professional help is received. It is not wrong or sinful to separate for reasons of physical and/or sexual abuse.

If the abuser continues his behavior and refuses to seek professional counseling, the woman should call a local shelter for battered women. A shelter is a safe place for a woman and her children to stay. Sometimes it takes legal action against the man, in the form of a restraining order, to begin to hold him accountable for his abusive actions. The woman should press charges

---

2. Notes from a lecture I gave on March 1, 1981. The concept of cyclical stages had been developed and adapted from the Domestic Abuse Project, Inc., of Minneapolis and Men in Violent Relationships, Inc., the latter of which I directed.

against the abuser if he refuses to show genuine remorse by seeking to make changes in his behavior and seeking professional counseling.

Sexual abuse, unwanted sexual action toward one's spouse, includes fondling sexual parts (breasts, buttocks, vaginal area, thighs, etc.) without permission or consent; forced intercourse; persistent, unwanted sexual touch while one's spouse is asleep; persistent, unwanted sexual innuendo; or unwanted, aggressive sexual behaviors that one spouse persistently performs on an unwilling spouse.

Struggling with Our Sinful Nature

Can you imagine the Father, Son, and Holy Spirit desanctifying each other? Why, then, do we desanctify each other in our marriages? Part of the answer lies in the fact that we still live in a fallen, sinful world. Even though we are Christians, we still sin. Romans 7:14–25 (NIVI) helps us to understand this:

> We know that the law is spiritual; but I am unspiritual, sold as a slave to sin. I do not understand what I do. For what I want to do I do not do, but what I hate I do. And if I do what I do not want to do, I agree that the law is good. As it is, it is no longer I myself who do it, but it is sin living in me. I know that nothing good lives in me, that is, in my sinful nature. For I have the desire to do what is good, but I cannot carry it out. For what I do is not the good I want to do; no, the evil I do not want to do—this I keep on doing. Now if I do what I do not want to do, it is no longer I who do it, but it is sin living in me that does it.
>
> So I find this law at work: When I want to do good, evil is right there with me. For in my inner being I delight in God's law; but I see another law at work in the members of my body, waging war against

the law of my mind and making me a prisoner of the law of sin at work within my members. What a wretched man I am! Who will rescue me from this body of death? Thanks be to God—through Jesus Christ our Lord!

So then, I myself in my mind am a slave to God's law, but in the sinful nature a slave to the law of sin.

This passage points out that all of us struggle internally between our old sinful natures and what God wants us to do through our new natures as Christians. Even the apostle Paul struggled greatly. We carry this same struggle into our marriages. Desanctifications are a direct result of our sinful nature. Let's look at one couple's story to better understand why we desanctify each other in marriage.

Self Talk Leading to Violence: Robert and Lois

Robert was a successful businessman and had reached the top in his company. He was hard-driving and likable, and so was his wife, Lois. Both found each other physically attractive, and they spent much time together.

Both came out of dysfunctional homes in which their needs for love and acceptance were not met. Instead, they had been wounded by the sting of criticism and the absence of praise. Lois and Robert both wanted love and acceptance, but because they never received this love and acceptance when they were growing up, they did not recognize love or acceptance when they did receive it. They told themselves, "Nobody loves me. My spouse doesn't love me, and my spouse never meets my needs." We can see these influences at work when we examine their marital self talk.

Robert's activating event was that Lois raised her voice. His self talk told him, "Why does she have to raise her voice? She knows I don't like this. If she loved me she wouldn't do this. She probably really doesn't love me." This made him feel hurt, rejected, and angry, so he was silent to Lois.

Robert's silence became Lois's activating event. Her self talk said, "He never shows me love. Everything I do fails with him. I'm so tired of this." She felt hurt, rejection, and anger, so she pushed Robert away and was verbally caustic to him.

Lois's verbal nastiness became Robert's next activating event. His self talk was, "She's so mean to me. She doesn't love me. I don't need her. I do need her. If I yell, she'll leave. If I don't yell, she'll keep yelling at me. I'm going to yell." Again he was hurt and angry, and he felt spiteful, so he yelled at Lois.

Robert's yelling was Lois's next activating event. She told herself, "He never listens to me. He never shows love to me. He never shows me acceptance. I just want love and acceptance, but he's yelling. I'll show him by kicking him—that'll make him stop yelling." She felt even more hurt, anger and resentment, so Lois yelled louder, swore at Robert, and kicked him in the leg.

The kick was Robert's third activating event. "I can't believe it, she kicked me," he thought. "She's out of control—she's lost her mind. I've got to stop this. I'll have to grab her to make her stop! I just want this to stop!" By now Robert was out of control, with high frustration and resentment. He grabbed Lois by the arm and swore at her.

This rapid downward spiraling occurred in a matter of moment. Their self talk intensified with each exchange, and as part of the intensification, they had more thoughts of desanctifying behaviors. Note that they thought this further desanctifying behavior would end the dispute. Their feelings and emotions intensified. Both of them were out of control, and each desanctified the other.

Robert and Lois are like buckets with holes in them (see fig. 15). No matter how many good feelings they try to pour into themselves, they can't pour in enough to feel whole and complete. Within their marriage they are codependent because they need each other to make them feel good about themselves, to fill the empty bucket. Since no person is able to fill completely another person, Robert and Lois live in misery because they don't feel loved and accepted by the other. During a conflict, these deep, unmet needs exacerbate their feelings of rejection and hurt. These unmet needs cause many of the fights; the desanctifying behaviors committed during the conflict lend credence to their distorted self talk, which intensifies on both sides and becomes a self-fulfilling prophecy. Their entropy is heightened because of their mutual mistrust and abuse.

Figure 15

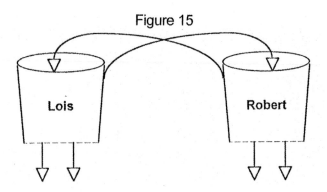

In summary, desanctifying behaviors don't make us feel good, but they also create further desanctifying behaviors. It is crucial to see them for what they are and to take steps to counter them, because they have such a negative effect on a marriage. In the midst of a conflict we must dispute our self talk and make sure we are seeing the true picture. It is here that we must keep our identities firmly in Christ and use his teachings to help us find better ways of dealing with conflicts. If desanctifying events occur persistently in your marriage, you can demonstrate your courage by seeking help from a counselor or a therapist.

Worksheet for You and Your Spouse

In the left column of the worksheet, list different types of desanctifying behavior and attitudes that you have had or done lately.

In the middle column of the worksheet, discuss the possible effects these attitudes and behaviors would have on your spouse.

In the right column, begin to identify healthier, sanctifying attitudes and behaviors toward your spouse.

Marital Desanctification Awareness Worksheet

My Types of Desanctifying Attitudes and Behaviors	Possible Impact on My Spouse	Healthier, Sanctifying Attitudes or Behaviors Toward My Spouse
1.		
2.		
3.		

©copyright 1992 by Brian Nystrom, LICSW, LMFT

Chapter opening quote is from *Minneapolis Star Tribune*, October 30, 1993, "When I Call for Help: A Pastoral Response to Domestic Violence Against Women," U. S. Catholic bishops.

Chapter 8

Sanctification:
Special and Set Apart

Do nothing out of selfish ambition or vain conceit, but in humility consider others better than yourselves. Each of you should look not only to your own interests, but also to the interests of others.

- Philippians 2:3–4 (NIVI)

In the last chapter we identified attitudes and behaviors that desanctify your spouse and increase entropy in your marriage. In this chapter, we will look at sanctifying attitudes and behaviors that will improve your marriage and make it stronger.

Remember that your thoughts produce your emotions and feelings and influence your behaviors. Improving your marriage lies first with your own thoughts and beliefs. As you work to examine your thoughts, your efforts will be rewarded with a relationship that is characterized by love, respect, openness, honesty, and trust. You will be able to more easily discuss the problems that do arise, because you and your spouse will have developed enough trust in each other's judgment and each other's love to share your concerns. And you will not have to worry about how things look on the outside, because you will be comfortable with who you are on the inside. You will be able to be more transparent with your spouse and with others.

Achieving this isn't easy. It takes courage, faith, and hard work (see fig. 16). Nor is it simple: our family issues are often unclear and overlapping; our self talk can lead us to incorrect conclusions and can cause us immeasurable pain. Learning to sanctify your spouse and your marriage is complex. This is why we have to take things in stages, learning and adapting, learning and practicing, learning and adapting some more.

Figure 16

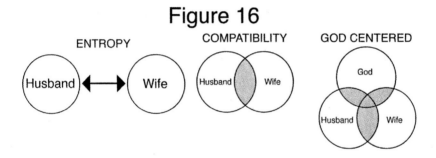

If you and your spouse become aware of desanctifications, then you need a plan to work them out. Pray for guidance and strength, and take the first steps toward a healthier marriage by making your spouse aware of the problem.

Becoming Aware of Desanctification

A primary goal of the PSR model of marriage is to be honest with your spouse and also to be open to what your spouse says to you. Our defenses and guards must be as low as possible through practicing our self talk. Try hard to hear what your spouse is really saying. Your spouse has the right to be honest with you, and if you want your spouse to hear you out, you must be prepared to do the same.

We also need to learn to empathize with our spouses to understand how the desanctification has affected them. To empathize means to put yourself in the place of your spouse emotionally and cognitively. Ask yourself, "How does my behavior affect my spouse?" When your spouse answers you, he or she may say things that you do not want to hear or that may be hard to accept, but it is critical that you listen. Ignoring your spouse is a powerful invalidation: it makes him or her feel isolated, frustrated, and unloved. It takes considerable energy to listen to another person at the same time you are learning to drop your defenses by disputing your distorted self talk and keeping a firm hand on your family influences. But with practice and God's help you can do this. Your reward for your hard work is that the level of entropy in your marriage will be lowered.

Once you are aware of the desanctification, you will feel *convicted* of the sin against your spouse. Your spouse is your equal. You ought to feel guilty when you sin against your spouse, whom you promised to love and cherish. The ideal marriage reflects the Trinity with the same degree of closeness. When you harm your spouse, you harm yourself.

Our consciences will sting us when we are made aware of our sin. As Romans 1:18–20 tells us, we know what is right and wrong. We know we are wrong when we have sinned, and our consciences will remind us if we try to ignore it.

For the wrath or God is revealed from heaven against all ungodliness and unrighteousness of men, who suppress the truth in unrighteousness, because that which is known about God is evident within them; for God made it evident to them. For since the creation of the world his invisible attributes, his eternal power and divine nature, have been clearly seen, being understood through what has been made, so that they are without excuse.

Once you become aware of your desanctification, you need to change your ways and *repent.* Depending on what the attitude or behavior was, this could be a lengthy process. If you have a persistent problem that you are unable to change alone, you may need to seek help. Try talking to others, such as a friend, a pastor, or a therapist, to understand the problem better. They might be able to suggest ways for you to deal with the problem.

To truly repent means we have to truly believe that what we have done is not right; otherwise we are merely going through the motions to placate our consciences and our spouses. This is a form of minimizing or denial. Falsely acknowledging a wrong will give a spouse the impression that we are sincere when we are not. Since our thoughts and beliefs fuel our behaviors, if we don't believe we are wrong, then we cannot truly repent. We have the greatest opportunity to change our lives if we use the deepest insight possible into our own behavior. Insight coupled with a godly love toward our spouses will build more authentic and life-changing attitudes and behaviors.

If we truly believe that we have desanctified our spouses, then we need to apologize and seek *forgiveness.* It is important to make the distinction as to who owns each of these behaviors: while we can apologize, only the wronged person can offer forgiveness. And apologizing to someone does not guarantee that we will be forgiven. We may need to allow that person to vent his or her feelings. The wronged person may need some time to gain perspective on what has happened. We cannot control this process without desanctifying someone once again. Give your spouse plenty of time and understanding, and you will reduce marital entropy. We do not have the right to impose on our spouses our standards of how long it should take to get over something. Instead, we need to analyze these personal standards to understand their origin.

If you have sinned against your spouse, forgiveness is between your spouse and God. The Holy Spirit will soften you, especially if your repentance is authentic. Your record with your spouse in these issues will likely be important in his or her consideration of forgiveness. In the past, have your efforts at repentance been sincere? Or have you faked repentance? If you have been insincere in the past, your spouse may be skeptical of the authenticity of your apology and repentance. If you have been sincere previously, then you might receive your spouse's authentic forgiveness in return.

Distorted thoughts produce desanctification of our spouses. Therefore, as we attempt to change our patterns of behavior toward our spouses, we must continually practice *cognitive restructuring* to reduce the possibility of future desanctifications.

Suppose we were to think, "It's okay to call my spouse a name," "It's okay to ignore my spouse," or "It's okay to invalidate my spouse." These statements are distorted, but if we do any of these things we must be telling ourselves that it is acceptable. Therefore, to change the behavior, we need to first identify, analyze, and dispute the distorted thought or belief that produced the behavior. We must each do this on a continuing, life-long basis to reduce desanctification and the resulting marital entropy. Negative thoughts will come to us during our lifetimes. The types and insensitivities will vary for each of us, depending on our unique histories, but we need to deal with them in the same way: see each negative thought for what it is, find out why it dropped in uninvited, and dispute it so we can send it on its way.

Sanctifying Your Spouse

We defined marital sanctification as treating our spouses so that they feel special and set apart. God's original design for marriage requires the kind of intimacy and compatibility imparted by sanctification. If our marriages are to reflect the Trinity, then we must be as close to one another as possible (Ephesians 5:26–27).

How do you sanctify your spouse? How do you create a marital sanctuary where your spouse will always feel safe, important, and special? How do you show your spouse that he or she is set apart, in a positive way, from everyone else you know? From the PSR model of marriage we know that treating our spouses this way is God's design, so these goals must be integrated into and entrenched in our belief systems.

We must first remember that wife and husband are equal partners under God. One does not rule over the other, as we saw in the sin era model of marriage. Believing in your spouse's equality and behaving accordingly has significant ramifications in the daily workings of marriage. Practicing the PSR model will increase marital sanctification and will decrease entropy. This requires energy. It is up to each of us to do our part to make our marriages work. The following guidelines will help you to recognize ways to base your marriage on the PSR model (see fig. 17).

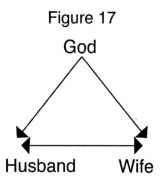

Figure 17

Joint decision making. Decisions about all aspects of the marriage and family flow through the partnership. This could include decisions about parenting, how your money is spent, or recreational or social activities. The couple talks everything out. If there is no consensual agreement, a decision should not be made and no action should be taken until there is consensual agreement. Unilateral decisions run contrary to God's words that "they shall rule together." *Marital sanctification occurs when both partners trust that they will be consulted on all decisions and that their opinions and desires are as important as their spouses'. Martial decisions are mutual decisions.*

Shared responsibility. The division of labor in a marriage should be about equal between husband and wife. We know that there are two kinds of work in marriage: work that generates income and work that does not generate income. The division of labor needs to take into account both kinds of work, so that the two kinds of labor are about equal between the spouses. A lopsided division of labor will cause resentment. For example, because the husband is the single or the major source of income does not mean he works harder than his wife does or that his work is worth more than hers. Cooking, doing laundry, cleaning, or juggling the children's schedules is much harder work than are many paid jobs outside the home. And the work should not end for the paid spouse when he or she comes home. Rather, an additional set of tasks faces the couple.

When I come home from the office, I will ask Mary Ann if she needs help with dinner preparations, house clean-up, or children's activities (homework, chores, transportation, baseball). We have to work together to make things flow as smoothly as possible.

Marital sanctification in this area occurs when both spouses know that they are contributing equally to the workload and that income-producing and nonincome-producing work are valued equally.

Nonthreatening behaviors. There must be an absence of any threatening or abusive behaviors. *Marital sanctification occurs when there are no threatening or abusive behaviors in the marriage.*

Economic partnership. Every paycheck, asset, or possession must be jointly owned between the spouses. There cannot be any economic secrets, such as clandestine savings accounts or information withheld from the other spouse. Every financial activity must be jointly discussed and mutually agreed on. Both spouses are responsible for knowing their joint financial picture and for keeping the other constantly apprised of anything that will change or affect that financial status. The couple has freedom to determine who will pay the bills, how to pay the bills and when, and how to funnel funds to different accounts to pay different bills. *Marital sanctification occurs when all income and assets are jointly held and there is continual sharing of financial information.*

Accountability and honesty. There must be a continual, two-way flow of information, revealing each spouse's feelings, thoughts, opinions, history, daily activities, future plans, goals, fears, likes, dislikes, and weaknesses. One spouse must not intentionally withhold information of any kind from the other spouse. Withholding information is deceptive. *Marital sanctification occurs when there is a continual, two-way flow of information without any form of deception.*

Parenting direction and decision making must be done on a mutual, agreed-upon basis for all matters. There can be no abuse or neglect of the children. Unilateral parenting decisions cause marital desanctification, because they remove one spouse from the mutual decision making necessary for a healthy marriage. Rough treatment will also cause marital desanctification. *Marital sanctification occurs when all aspects of parenting are done mutually or by mutual agreement and the children are treated lovingly and respectfully.*

Validation. There is a continual effort made to understand and empathize with each other in order to validate the other spouse's perception of reality. This means we take our spouse's opinions, comments, feelings, likes, dislikes, ideas, perspectives, and wants seriously. Minimizing or denying contributes to marital desanctification. *Marital sanctification occurs when there is an environment of mutual validation and an absence of invalidation.*

Trust and commitment. We must place high value on our spouses as people and on the sanctity of our marriage. Ridiculing, lecturing, threatening to leave or divorce, making demands or judgments, invalidating, using pornography, having affairs, flirting, abusing drugs or alcohol, maintaining poor hygiene, using poor etiquettes or language all devalue the other spouse. *Marital sanctification occurs as the other spouse feels the high value placed on the relationship on an ongoing, lifetime basis.*

Fairness and lack of demands. There is a constant balancing of fairness between the spouses in the relationship. There would never be a demand placed on one spouse at the expense of another. *Marital sanctification occurs in an environment void of demands with an emphasis on fairness toward the other spouse's wants and needs.*

Edification and encouragement. Both spouses demonstrate mutual encouragement and general care and respect for the other, and both spouses make positive efforts to build up the other. Marital desanctification occurs when one spouse degrades, invalidates, ridicules, yells at, or verbally abuses the other spouse. *Marital sanctification occurs where there is an ongoing state of mutual encouragement, edification, respect, and care shown for the other in the marriage.*

Spiritual and social relationships. There is respect and encouragement in terms of each one's relationship with Jesus Christ and social relationships with others. Attempts to isolate a spouse from friends or family or to control his or her worship of God by controlling specific church selection are desanctifying and abusive. Ridicule, discouragement, or condescension regarding these areas is stifling and abusive. *Marital sanctification occurs when freedom, respect, and encouragement are shown to the other's journey with Jesus Christ and his or her social support groups.*

Questions for You and Your Spouse to Answer and Discuss

1. Do you believe desanctifications are wrong? Why, or why not?
2. Have you apologized to your spouse for desanctifications? How?

Homework for You and Your Spouse

Listed below are the eleven areas of a marriage that reflects the PSR model. Consider your marriage and discuss with your spouse whether you sanctify or desanctify your spouse in each area. Identify any changes that you need to make.

Joint decision making

Shared responsibility

Nonthreatening behaviors

Economic partnership

Accountability and honesty

Parenting

Validation

Trust and commitment

Fairness and lack of demands

Edification and encouragement

Spiritual and social relationships

Chapter 9

Blocking Entropy: Communication

No one can tame the tongue. It is a restless evil, full of deadly poison.
- James 3:8 (NIVI)

Fools find no pleasure in understanding but delight in airing their own opinions.
- Proverbs 18:2 (NIVI)

Dialogue is to love what blood is to the body. When the flow of blood stops in your body the body dies. And when the flow of dialogue stops between a husband and a wife the relationship dies.
- Dr. Paul Faulkner

Communication is the lifeblood of a marriage—with it, compatibility and intimacy are enhanced; without it, a marriage will suffer.

Communication means many different things to different people. We have learned that each of us brings a set of beliefs and attitudes about communication into a marriage, and these family beliefs depend on what we learned when we were growing up. We learned certain rules and expectations about how to express ourselves. Some of us also learned what not to say, for fear of punishment or rejection.

We all make noise from the instant we are born, and we talk most of our lives. You might think that we then know how to communicate with one another, but this is not the case. How often has your spouse misinterpreted something you've said? How many arguments have begun over a misunderstanding? How often have you held your tongue because you didn't know how to say something? Most of us need to improve our communication skills, and some of us need to learn them.

Paul and Lisa, whom we met in chapter 4, are a good example of how poor communication can affect a marriage. In Paul's family, doing a good job was the minimum acceptable standard. He assumed Lisa thought the way he did, and because he never expected to be complimented, he never complimented or praised his wife. To Lisa, it seemed that everyone was praiseworthy except her.

Self talk is vital in good marital communication because it is the basis of what we say to our spouses. Paul's distorted beliefs caused him to withhold praise and approval from Lisa. She didn't feel safe, because everything she did was fuel for his ridicule. Paul's most fundamental assumptions and beliefs about relationships were invisible to him. He had no idea of their negative impact on Lisa, and he didn't recognize how they increased the entropy in his marriage.

It is also obvious that our marital interactive self talk influences our communication. By reacting unthinkingly to the other person's words and behaviors, your interactive self talk about your spouse can be pushed into a downward spiral of negativity.

Our identities in Christ are also an integral part of our communication. If we have a destructive, distorted view of ourselves, without the anchor of knowing who we are in Christ, this will obstruct healthy communication.

Finally, the PSR model of marriage will have an impact on the quality of communication in your marriage. If you see marriage as a partnership, you will view each other differently than if you see marriage as a hierarchy. If both spouses are equal, of one flesh, and have the goal of sanctifying each other, think how different the communication will be in comparison with that in other models.

Communication means sharing things with your spouse, listening and responding to what he or she says in a way that fosters marital sanctification. An important part of communication is transparency, which means revealing to your spouse as much as is possible and appropriate on an ongoing basis. When you are transparent with your spouse, there is nothing—such as your defenses, misunderstandings, mistaken assumptions, untruths, or deceptions—in the way.

Levels of Communication Transparency

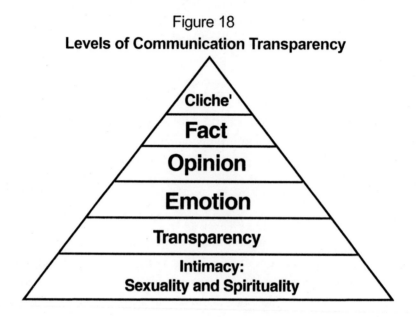

Figure 18
Levels of Communication Transparency

Cliche'
Fact
Opinion
Emotion
Transparency
Intimacy:
Sexuality and Spirituality

There are six levels of communication transparency (see fig. 18), and the lowest level, *cliché,* is communication merely intended to acknowledge another person or break the silence. Much of our communication is nonverbal, so our physical gestures, such as nodding or waving, can also be clichés. Clichés reveal little about who we are.

At the level of *fact,* we share information with each other. This kind of communication shows what you know, assuming that what you know is correct.

When we share *opinions*, we begin to share part of ourselves with another person. Sharing an opinion means sharing a perspective or viewpoint on something, based on our analysis of the situation. When we give an opinion, we show each other more about who we are, because this involves an integration of fact and judgment that is uniquely ours. This makes interactions more interesting, but it is here that we must also begin to exercise caution. Opinions are just that—opinions. We must not impose our opinions onto our spouses. Attempting to force an opinion on someone is an abusive, unabashed power play.

The level of *emotion* involves sharing our feelings and emotions, and at this level we are becoming more transparent with each other about who we are as people. For example, if you tell your spouse, "I feel hurt when you walk away from me," you have sent a message and let your spouse know more about you as a person.

Your emotions, however, are yours. If you are angry, the anger belongs to you. No one made you angry. Although someone else's behavior can be an activating event that triggers your emotions, you have the ability to choose how you feel. If you carefully evaluate your self talk and examine why you feel angry, you might be able to divert that emotion into positive energy. Pause, take a deep breath, and dispute your self talk. Make sure you understand what you are reacting to. Then you can honestly say what you are feeling, and you can do that without making things worse. Instead of yelling, "Why do you throw your dirty clothes on the floor every night? I spend all day cleaning and you don't care!" try saying, "I feel angry and frustrated when you don't put things where they belong. It makes me think you don't respect the effort it takes me to keep the house clean." If you can say this quietly and calmly, the issue will remain the clothes on the floor. Your spouse has a right to know how you feel about things. If you hide the messages, she or he may never know who you are.

Being *transparent* within your marriage means sharing everything about yourself, including facts, opinions, feelings and emotions, likes and dislikes, weaknesses and strengths, goals, future plans, aspirations, fears, history, and thoughts. This helps your spouse to know you as a person, and it generates compatibility and intimacy in the relationship.

For all of us there are obstacles to being transparent, but we need to work at identifying and removing the obstacles. For example, an obstacle could be a fear of rejection or abandonment, lack of communication skills, or high entropy in the marriage. We may tend to avoid being transparent, even with those closest to us, because most of us can recall a time we have been hurt by sharing with someone who didn't value the gift we were giving. Part of the special kind of trust that grows between spouses is the trust that your spouse will not take advantage of the vulnerability you show when you dare to be transparent. Transparency shows that you are willing to be authentic with your spouse, and that makes your spouse feel special, trusted, and valued.

> Do not lie to each other, since you have taken off your old self with its practices and have put on the new self, which is being renewed in knowledge in the image of its Creator. Here there is no Greek or Jew, circumcised and uncircumcised, barbarian, Scythian, slave and free, but Christ is all, and is in all. (Colossians 3:9-11 NIVI)

> Therefore each of you must put off falsehood and speak truthfully to your neighbor, for we are all members of one body. (Ephesians 4:25 NIVI)

Intimacy is a deeper level of transparency that incorporates both spirituality and sexuality. Spiritual transparency involves revealing to your spouse the nature and essence of your ongoing relationship with God. Sexual transparency involves revealing to your spouse the essence of your sexual being and then interacting in a loving, sexual way without imposing your will or desanctifying your spouse. You should be able to do this free of shame or embarrassment, as a natural part of who you are with your spouse.

If you can share transparency and intimacy with your spouse, you will both reveal to each other who you really are. As you come to truly know one another, it is natural to implement the guidelines for marital sanctification (chapter 8).

Not surprisingly, we are transparent with very few individuals. There is an inverse relationship between transparency and the number of people with whom we are transparent.

Sexual intimacy should be reserved for the marriage relationship only. An affair or romance is a desanctification that will affect trust for a long, long time, if not permanently. And an affair will never solve marital problems.

Our thoughts about God, our petitions for help, or our instances of seeking guidance and strength are so well hidden that almost no one knows what is happening between us and God. Most marriages do not have spiritual transparency between spouses; may have nothing even close to it. The majority of couples rarely pray intimately together. It is necessary to identify the obstacles to spiritual transparency in order to share this kind of connectedness with your spouse.

As we continue to take on the mind of Christ, it is essential to reconfigure our thoughts to ideas and beliefs that correspond to our new identity. We need to know more about biblical, Christ-like ideas and concepts that will help us balance the distortions that we have about marriage and relationships. Merely reciting a Bible verse will not change a person. I believe that God's Word, coupled with the Holy Spirit and our desire to change, will create an attitude of wanting to identify entropy increasers—and then change them.

Active Listening and Communication

Active listening and communication means communication that is more than just one person talking. You must actively, and with energy, engage the other person as she or he communicates to gain understanding and empathy. Observe body language, facial expressions, and volume and tone of voice. At the same time, filter what you are hearing through the grid of everything you already know about your spouse in order to effectively analyze what you hear. You may need to ask more questions in order to understand.

We are all capable of listening effectively, but the things we've already discussed—distorted self talk and beliefs, dysfunctional family influences, un undeveloped identity in Christ, dysfunctional marital self talk and marital desanctification—increase entropy and are roadblocks to effective communication.

Also, listening actively requires your energy and effort on a continuing basis. (Remember what Johnny Carson said about giving his energy to his work instead of to marriage.) A healthy marriage marked by transparency, active listening, and good communication energizes you, because it frees you of bondage. Staying dysfunctional requires an enormous amount of energy. Why not channel that energy into healthy patterns?

Finally, although we all seem to know how to talk, not all of us know how to listen. You can learn and practice communication skills.

State your feelings. It is much better to say "I feel" instead of "you make me feel." Saying the latter sounds like you are blaming the other person, and it will likely be an activating event that causes defensiveness in the other person. Think carefully about the thoughts that are producing the feelings and attempt to connect the two. It is okay to present so-called negative emotions such as anger and displeasure. Many times it is difficult to share anger with others because we are not sure of how the other person will feel. The emotions are okay; what matters is how we express them.

> "In your anger do not sin": Do not let the sun go down while you are still angry, and do not give the devil a foothold. (Ephesians 4:26–27 NIVI)

Listen without interrupting. Listen while your spouse talks, not only to the words that are spoken but also to the words that aren't spoken. Watch your spouse's body language. Do not speak until your spouse is finished. This can be difficult at times, but interrupting your spouse shows disrespect.

> Those who guard their mouths and their tongues keep themselves from calamity. (Proverbs 21:23 NIVI)

> Those who lack judgment deride their neighbors, but those who have insight hold their tongues. (Proverbs 11:12 NIVI)

> To answer before listening—that is folly and shame. (Proverbs 18:13 NIVI)

Compliments and praise. Build up your spouse! Find the good things about your spouse and your relationship and acknowledge them to your spouse directly. The idea that we should not give praise is a distortion. Many of us grew up in families in which we were not praised, and therefore we never learned how to praise. I believe that Satan does not want us to praise our spouses, because valid praise strengths us individually and as married couples. You can learn to praise and compliment your spouse.

> Therefore encourage one another and build each other up, just as in fact you are doing. (1 Thessalonians 5:11 NIVI)

Do not let any unwholesome [rotten] talk come out of your mouths, but only what is helpful for building others up according to their needs, that it may benefit those who listen. (Ephesians 4:29 NIVI)

Note that Ephesians 4:29 says "according to their needs." Your spouse's needs shift and change frequently. By paying attention to this we give grace to our spouse and produce marital sanctification.

Be kind. Just be nice to your spouse. Use kind, encouraging words. This makes the home and marriage a refuge in which to regroup from the stress and strain of living.

Be kind and compassionate to one another, forgiving each other, just as in Christ God forgave you. (Ephesians 4:32 NIVI)

Give undivided attention. Focus your time, energy, and attention on your spouse. This shows that you are interested in your spouse and are trying to understand what is going to be said. This may mean stopping whatever you are doing: putting down the paper or turning down the television. It is often easier to be preoccupied by what we want or what we are doing than it is to give someone our undivided attention.

Investigate and probe. In order to make certain that you understand what your spouse is saying, you may need to ask nonthreatening questions. Ask about his or her feelings, daily activities, goals, frustrations, or plans. Each response may elicit another question from you. Remember that your spouse is a unique individual with many complexities, which you'll need to explore. Notice (**cartoon 3**) Mrs. Lockhorn has no interest in investigating Leroy's thoughts and feelings.

The Lockhorns / By William Hoest

"That's the way I see it. And now, Leroy will tell you the way he'd better see it."

Open-ended questions. An open-ended question allows your spouse latitude and freedom in answering your question. It will help enrich the discussion. Asking "How was your day?" instead of "Was your day okay?" elicits more information. There is a balance; eventually we need to be more specific, depending on the nature of the discussion.

Think before you speak. Remember to evaluate your self talk for distortions, and dispute any distortions that you find.

> Those who guard their lips guard their lives, but those who speak rashly will come to ruin. (Proverbs 13:3 NIVI)

> The wise in heart are called discerning, and pleasant words promote instruction. (Proverbs 16:21 NIVI)

Take an interest in your spouse. Focus your conversation on what is of interest to your spouse. Often we can be self-absorbed, focusing on ourselves instead of on the other person. We can ask our spouses about our daily routines, who they talked with, what's new in their lives, or their views on various topics. This requires energy.

> Do nothing out of selfish ambition or vain conceit, but in humility consider others better than yourselves. Each of you should look not only to your own interests, but also to the interests of others. Your attitude should be the same as that of Jesus Christ. (Philippians 2:3–5 NIVI)

Paraphrase/replay. To paraphrase means to repeat what you have just heard your spouse say without adding any editorials, criticisms, or judgments. This requires concentration on what your spouse is saying to you and will therefore cause you to pay attention. But it also gives evidence to your spouse that you are truly attempting to listen. Part of the purpose of paraphrasing is to find out if you are hearing and understanding your spouse accurately. If you paraphrase inaccurately, this gives your spouse an opportunity to clarify what he or she just said. You'll know you have understood your spouse completely when you paraphrase a remark and your spouse says "that's right" or "exactly."

Just because you accurately paraphrase a remark doesn't mean you are agreeing with it. What you are looking for is agreement on the content of your spouse's statement. After you are sure of the content, then you can respond to it.

Pause. Wait a few seconds before responding. This helps avoid reactiveness by slowing down the conversation. It gives both spouses an opportunity to think things through and to be aware of their self talk. It is particularly important to pause if you are angry or if the situation is at a critical point. The extra moment may allow you to gain control of your tongue and avoid saying something you will both regret.

Assess the Situation. Assessing the situation on a scale of one to ten is a simple technique to use when you are attempting to determine your spouse's level of interest on a given item. You might say, "On a scale of one to ten, rate your desire for Chinese take-out tonight." Your spouse responds, "Chinese food is a six, but Italian is a nine." You say, "Hmmm. I'd give Italian a six and Chinese a five. How about calling for a pizza?" Both spouses have clarified their current levels of interest in Chinese versus Italian food, and they've settled the issue of what to have for dinner tonight. They've also avoided the what-do-you-want-to-do-I-don't-know-what-do-you-want-to-do routine. The same question asked on a different night could produce different results, so it's important to check and not to make assumptions.

Volley the conversation. Keep the conversation lively by asking questions, paraphrasing what you have heard, or introducing new considerations. A conversation is like a tennis game in which players volley the ball back and forth. The longer the volley, the more interesting the game.

Be aware of voice. Be aware of the volume, pitch, and tone of your voice and aim for moderation. Just because you come form a family of yellers doesn't make it okay to yell in your marriage. Consider the effect these components have on communication.

Action love. Show your love through your verbal and physical actions. Don't hold back or assume that your spouse doesn't want it. We all need several doses daily. Action love is an integration of all the previous active listening skills.

Dear friends, let us love one another, for love comes from God. Everyone who loves has been born of God and knows God. Whoever does not love does not know God, because God is love. This is how God showed his love among us: He sent his one and only Son into the world so that we might live through him. This is love: not that we loved God, but that he loved us and sent his Son as an atoning sacrifice for our sins. Dear friends, since God so loved us, we also ought to love one another. (1 John 4:7–11 NIVI)

But the fruit of the Spirit is love, joy, peace, patience, kindness, goodness, faithfulness, gentleness and self-control. Against such things there is no law. (Galatians 5:22–23 NIVI)

And over all these virtues put on love, which binds them all together in perfect unity. Let the peace of Christ rule in your hearts, since as members of one body you were called to peace. And be thankful. (Colossians 3:14–15 NIVI)

Make it clear that your spouse is an important person. This is an attitude that incorporates the PSR model of marriage, in which you see your spouse as valuable, important, equal to you, and made in the image of God. Therefore you would not want your actions or words to desanctify your spouse. This guiding principle begins to take root in your attitudes, ideas, and opinions, and it is then displayed in the manner in which you treat your spouse.

Finally, all of you, live in harmony with one another; be sympathetic, love one another, be compassionate and humble. Do not repay evil with evil or insult with insult, but with blessing, because to this you were called so that you may inherit a blessing. For,
"Whoever among you would love life
    and see good days
must keep your tongue from evil

and your lips from deceitful speech.
Turn from evil and do good;
    seek peace and pursue it.
For the eyes of the Lord are on the righteous
    and his ears are attentive to their prayer,
But the face of the Lord is against those who do evil" (1 Peter 3:8–12 NIVI)

Consult with your spouse. Consulting with your spouse means checking things out with each other before acting—it does not mean seeking permission. As partners, you value each other's opinions, so it is natural that you would want to bounce your ideas off the other person. If the matter under consideration is an important one, it would be better to delay making a decision if you cannot reach an agreement. Consider that your spouse is your best ally, and he or she may think of things that you have not. Talking about alternatives, options, timing, and other considerations will help bring out the most balanced perspective and decision.

> Plans fail for lack of counsel, but with many advisers they succeed. (Proverbs 15:22 NIVI)

> Good understanding wins favor, but the way of the unfaithful is hard. All who are prudent act out of knowledge, but fools expose their folly. (Proverbs 13:15–16 NIVI)

Conversational prayer. To engage in conversational prayer means to be able to talk about God and your spirituality with your spouse and to pray with your spouse. Spiritual transparency means to share these things with your spouse on an ongoing basis. It also means answering your spouse's questions and concerns about these areas.

> Pray continually; give thanks in all circumstances, for this is God's will for you in Christ Jesus. (1 Thessalonians 5:17–18 NIVI)

Therefore confess your sins to each other and pray for each other so that you may be healed. The prayer of a righteous person is powerful and effective. (James 5:16 NVI)

And do not get drunk with wine, for that is dissipation, but be filled with the Spirit, speaking to one another in psalms and hymns and spiritual songs, singing and making melody with your heart to the Lord; always giving thanks for all things in the name of our Lord Jesus Christ to God, even the Father; and be subject to one another in the fear of Christ. (Ephesians 5:18–21 NASB)

Shift your demands to desires. In your self talk, try to continually shift demands to desires so that you don't make unspoken ultimatums. This will lessen your anger and frustration with your spouse and others. This helps create flexibility in our thinking and responses. It also makes you easier and more pleasant to converse with.

Visualize your family. This process involves thinking about your spouse and children as much as you can prior to seeing them. Visualizing helps to develop a mental and emotional connection with them, yielding empathy and receptivity to them when you do see them. This principle will help you to tune into your family's needs more quickly and foster a close relationship. You might try visualizing your spouse and children and think about their day. This helps you to think about things they have done during the day, which in turn creates empathy and connectedness with them.

Validate your spouse. To validate your spouse means to accept and acknowledge your spouse's viewpoints, opinions, thoughts, desires, or aspirations, even if you don't agree with them. This powerful concept stems from the PSR model of marriage. Validating your spouse forces you to come out of your self-absorption and focus on the other person. It takes energy.

A gentle answer turns away wrath, but a harsh word stirs up anger. The tongue of the wise commends knowledge acceptable, but the mouth of the fool gushes folly. (Proverbs 15:1–2 NIVI)

Questions for You and Your Spouse to Answer and Discuss

1. What obstacles to transparency do you have?
2. How would reducing these obstacles and being more transparent with your spouse benefit you?
3. Which active listening skills do you need to develop or practice?
4. How could you incorporate your answer to the third question into your marriage each day?
5. How can you incorporate these active listening skills into your communication style with your children?

Chapter opening quote is from Dr. Paul Faulkner, *How to Kill Communication*, film on marriage, from session 5.

Epilogue

My hope and prayer is that the material presented in this book has benefited you. There is a lot of material, so you may want to reread certain sections. Answer the questions at the end of each chapter; discuss them with your spouse and your friends. Challenge each other to apply the principles. Apply active listening skills during the discussion.

Remember not to aim for a perfect marriage, since that's impossible. Work instead toward a relationship in which you continually identify entropy and eliminate it whenever possible. You are a complex person, and marriage exponentially heightens the complex interactions between two people who are partners for a lifetime. I believe that by applying the principles and materials in this book, you can find greater compatibility and intimacy.

You have learned about many principles and ways to improve your marriage while decreasing entropy in it. Think about these, practice them, and over time you will see changes in yourself and in your marriage. Ordinary people—all of us—can have extraordinary marriages by reclaiming God's original design for oneness in marriage. God's blessings on you in your marriage journey.

Appendix

Finding a Marriage Counselor

If your marriage needs the intervention of a marriage counselor, please don't think of it as a failure. If our cars break down, or if something breaks in our homes, we call a mechanic or a repairperson. When it comes to marriage, however, our denial and pride can get in the way. Our cultural myths tell us that marriage is easy and everybody ought to be able to have a wonderful marriage, but the high divorce rate shows that's nonsense. Don't let your marriage deteriorate for lack of help. If you need the help of a competent therapist, you will want to consider at least four areas.

Credentials

Ideally you will want to find a licensed marriage and family therapist (LMFT). An LMFT has graduate training in marriage and family therapy and has several years of experience in this field. Other types of professionals can help you but an LMFT specializes in this area.

Like LMFTs, clinical social workers and psychologists have graduate training and can treat marriage and family issues. They may also specialize in other areas, such as emotional problems, depression, anxiety disorders, or eating disorders. They should be licensed at the highest levels by their state's licensing agency.

A psychiatrist, a medical doctor with special training in mental disorders, usually does not handle marriage and family therapy. Most of their work involves the prescription of psychotropic drugs to treat such disorders as depression or anxiety.

If you go to a mental health clinic, make sure that the clinic is licensed by your state to ensure quality and the protection of your rights. Every state will have different guidelines. Licensing gives a clinic credibility and helps to ensure that at least the minimal standards of quality care are in effect. You will find most types of mental health professionals organized in a clinic.

Nonlicensed psychotherapists, counselors, pastors, and others also offer therapy of many different kinds. Most states do not regulate these persons. Make sure that you check on their backgrounds and determine if they are supervised. Find out if complaints have been filed against them. Some states have boards or agencies that act as clearinghouses for registering complaints of this type. If the person is licensed, call his or her licensing board (look in the phone book or ask the therapist for the phone number) and ask if the therapist has had any complaints filed or any disciplinary actions taken against him or her. I would avoid counselors in this category unless you have strong evidence that they are qualified and experienced in therapy.

Experience

For all the therapists you are considering, ask how long they have been practicing marital therapy and if they have ever worked with a case similar to yours. The more experience they have, the better they can help you. I think it is helpful if the therapist is married, because that gives the therapist the unique perspective of understanding what marriage is about. You want to find a competent, seasoned therapist, so don't be bashful about asking these questions. You have a right to the answers.

Cost

Ask about the hourly rate and other fees. A well-run clinic will have all of this in writing for you on you first visit, and you can also get this information over the phone. Sometimes your medical insurance will pay for part of the cost if the marriage problems are producing emotional problems or making existing problems worse. Insurance companies use the medical model when they determine what costs they will cover. This means that there has to be a diagnosable problem, such as depression, that can be treated through the proposed marital therapy.

Even if you have to pay for the therapy, it is worth the investment, and it costs less than the fees for a divorce attorney. Your marriage is worth the cost of counseling. Many clinics will adjust their rates, based on the person's income level, if the person is paying for therapy out of pocket.

Christian Values

A competent Christian marriage therapist will be ideal for Christian clients, but finding this combination can be difficult. When you are considering therapists, ask how they integrate Christian principles into their counseling. Determine their views of marriage, divorce, and so on. A competent secular marriage therapist can be used if a competent Christian therapist cannot be found.

How to Find a Therapist

Word of mouth is an effective way to find a therapist. Ask friends or people that you trust if they know of a therapist who has helped them. Your pastor or relatives may know of a therapist. Some medical insurance companies will refer you to therapists in your area. Your employer may offer an Employee Assistance Program (EAP) that will assess your needs and make a referral to a therapist or a clinic. Often the assessment is free, and it is nearly always guaranteed to be confidential—employers are not told which employees sought help for what. You can also look in the yellow pages of your phone book for a listing of professionals under "counseling" or "Marriage/Family." These ads can be a helpful source of information about credentials, licensure, cost, location, and specialties.

Notes

Recommended Reading

Self Talk

Backus, William. *Telling Yourself the Truth*. Minneapolis: Bethany House, 1980.

Beck, Aaron. *Love Is Never Enough*. New York: Harper Perennial, 1988.

Beck, Aaron et al. *Cognitive Therapy of Depression*. New York: Guildford Press, 1979.

Yankura, Joseph, and Windy Dryden. *Doing RET: Albert Ellis in Action*. New York: Springer, 1990.

Male-Female Biblical Equality

Bilezikian, Gilbert. *Beyond Sex Roles: What the Bible Says about a Woman's Place in Church and Family*. Grand Rapids, Mich.: Baker, 1986.

Elasky Fleming, Joy, with J. Robin Maxson. Man and Woman in Biblical Unity: Theology from Genesis 2-3. Minneapolis: Christians for Biblical Equality, 1993.

Hull, Gretchen Gaebelein. *Equal to Serve: Women and Men Working Together Revealing the Gospel.* Baker Books, 1998.

Groothuis, Rebecca Merrill. *Good News for Women: A Biblical Picture of Gender Equality.* Baker Books, 1997.

Domestic Violence

Kroeger, Catherine Clark and James R. Beck. *Women, Abuse, and the Bible: How Scripture Can Be Used to Hurt or Heal.* Baker Books, 1996.

Alsdurf, James and Phyllis. *Battered into Submission: The Tragedy of Wife Abuse in the Christian Home.* Wipf and Stock, 1998.

Shame and Grace

Bradshaw, John. *Healing the Shame that Binds You.* Deerfield Beach, Fla.: Health Communications, 1988.

VanVonderan, Jeff. *Families Where Grace Is in Place.* Minneapolis: Bethany House, 1992.

———. *Tired of Trying to Measure Up.* Minneapolis: Bethany House, 1989.

Spiritual Abuse

Blue, Ken. *Healing Spiritual Abuse: How to Break Free from Bad Church Experiences*. Downers Grove, Ill.: InterVarsity Press, 1993.

Johnson, Dave, and Jeff VanVonderan. *The Subtle Power of Spiritual Abuse*. Minneapolis: Bethany House, 1991.

Addiction

Carnes, Patrick. *Out of the Shadows: Understanding Sexual Addiction*. Minneapolis: CompCare, 1985.

Johnson, Vernon. *I'll Quit Tomorrow*. San Francisco: Harper and Row, 1980.

Spickard, Anderson, and Barbara R. Thompson. *Dying for a Drink: What You should Know about Alcoholism*. Dallas: Word, 1986.

Codependency

Beatty, Melodie. *Beyond Co-dependency: And Getting Better All the Time*. San Francisco: Harper and Row, 1989.

_____. *Co-dependent No More: How to Stop Controllnig Others and Start Caring for Yourself*. San Francisco: Harper and Row, 1987.

If you would like to express your ideas, please write to:

Life Resources America, Inc.
Brighton Professional Building
1900 Silver Lake Road, #110
St. Paul, MN 55112

You can also order this book and many other Christian-based self-help and recovery books, audiotapes, videotapes, and other products by writing to us or by calling our toll-free number:

1-800-406-9727

or by faxing:

1-651-628-0411

www.nystromcounseling.com

Glossary

Activating event: a situation or circumstance that triggers one's thoughts. It can be anything that gets things going—a song on the radio, conflict with one's spouse, driving (chapter 3).

Atmosphere of safety: an environment in which it is safe to be authentic and to discuss anything in a transparent way with another person. The atmosphere is free from every type of desanctification.

Behaviors: actions caused by one's thoughts, such as talking, avoidance, speeding, or overeating. The key to changing any behavior is to change one's thoughts (chapter 3).

Belief: a conviction produced in part by one's family. Beliefs are part of our self talk (chapter 3). *See also* Self talk.

Codependency: a relationship in which one person needs the other person to provide approval and validation in order to feel good about himself or herself. It is a draining relationship that lacks maturity (chapters 2–4).

Cognitions: thoughts (chapter 3).

Cognitive restructuring: changing or reframing one's thoughts so one looks at things a different way. Since thoughts produce emotions and behavior, it is only by first restructuring one's cognitions that one can change emotions or behaviors (chapter 3).

Consequences: the effects of an action or thought. Behaviors, feelings, and emotions are the consequences of thoughts (chapter 3).

Cycle: a dynamic pattern in one's self talk, emotions, and behaviors that repeats itself in a predictable way.

Desanctification: a destructive behavior by which one's spouse is harmed by poor treatment (chapter 7).

Disputation: the active process of challenging one's thoughts and comparing them with a Christian model to test the truth or balance in them (chapters 3–4).

Dysfunction(al): attitudes or behaviors that disrupt or impede a healthy role for oneself in a marriage or in a family (chapters 1–2).

Edification: active behavior aimed at building up, improving, or encouraging one's spouse (chapters 6 and 8).

Entropy, marital: disorder; deterioration of the bonds resulting from lack of energy contributed by one or both marital partners (chapter 1).

Entropy catalyst or increaser: anything that stimulates or prolongs entropy in a marriage (chapter 1).

Family of origin: the family in which one grows up; in this book, referred to as family or upbringing. One's family has its own culture, communication style, expectations, and problems that shape each person. Parts of one's family are healthy; other parts are not. Unhealthy family influences catalyze or increase entropy (chapter 2).

Feelings and emotions: internal consequences of one's thoughts, such as resentment, anger, hurt, happiness, joy, or contentment (chapter 3).

Frame: a person's unique interpretation of a given situation or circumstance (chapters 3–4).

Garden of Eden model of marriage: God's original design for marriage in which Adam and Eve were equal partners (chapter 6). *See also* Partnership-service-regency (PSR) model of marriage and Genesis 2.

Identification: the process of isolating thoughts and labeling them if they are irrational, distorted, or negative (chapters 3–4).

Invalidation: verbalizations or behaviors that degrade, deny, or tear down one's spouse, whether done intentionally or unintentionally. Invalidations begin with one's self talk and flow into one's actions (chapters 7–9).

Marital self talk: self talk produced in a marital interaction, in which one spouse reacts internally to the verbalizations or behaviors of the other spouse (chapter 4).

Paradigm: a person's unique model, or grid, that causes a person to interpret information in a certain way (chapter 3).

Partnership-service-regency (PSR) model of marriage: a return to God's original design for marriage, characterized by submission to God and equality between the spouses (chapter 6).

Partnership: a legal term denoting equality of ownership. In a marriage, partners are of equal rank. The marriage partners "rule together" (Genesis 2) (chapter 6).

Redemption era model of marriage: a return to God's original design for marriage that is made possible by Jesus Christ being the perfect sacrifice for our sins (chapter 6). *See also* Partnership-service-regency model of marriage.

Reactionary cycling: familiar activating events that trigger a spouse's thoughts and produce a reaction, which in turn triggers the other spouse's thoughts and produces another reaction, in a predictable cycle (chapter 4).

Reframing: reinterpreting a situation or circumstance as a result of disputing one's self talk (chapters 3–4).

Regency: to rule; "they shall rule together" (Genesis 2). The couple rules together, in an integrated way, instead of in an isolated fashion (chapter 6).

Sanctification: the active process of loving and treating one's spouse in such a fashion that he or she feels special and set apart in a positive way (chapters 6 and 8).

Self talk: one's internal running commentary of words, ideas, beliefs, concepts, observations, opinions, or perspectives. One's self talk may be positive or negative (chapter 3).

Service: the energetic, positive process of providing usefulness and value to one's spouse through communication, action, love and sanctification (chapters 6 and 8). *See also* Partnership-service-regency model of marriage.

Sin era model of marriage: marriage subverted by the consequences of the original sin (chapter 6).

Transparency: the ability to be open and honest in a human relationship such that spouses can see and know as much about one another as possible. This involves the active process of removing as many obstacles as possible (chapter 8-9).

Validation: verbalizations or behaviors that confirm the value of one's spouse's opinions, values, and actions, whether one agrees with them or not. Validation begins in one's self talk and flows into one actions and behaviors (chapter 8-9).

Printed in the United States
19888LVS00006B/469-504